3

READING
EXPLORER

THIRD EDITION

NANCY DOUGLAS

DAVID BOHLKE

NATIONAL GEOGRAPHIC
LEARNING

Australia · Brazil · Mexico · Singapore · United Kingdom · United States

National Geographic Learning,
a Cengage Company

Reading Explorer 3
Third Edition

Nancy Douglas and David Bohlke

Publisher: Andrew Robinson

Executive Editor: Sean Bermingham

Senior Development Editor: Christopher Street

Director of Global Marketing: Ian Martin

Heads of Regional Marketing:

Charlotte Ellis (Europe, Middle East and Africa)

Kiel Hamm (Asia)

Irina Pereyra (Latin America)

Product Marketing Manager: Tracy Bailie

Senior Production Controller: Tan Jin Hock

Associate Media Researcher: Jeffrey Millies

Art Director: Brenda Carmichael

Operations Support: Hayley Chwazik-Gee

Manufacturing Planner: Mary Beth Hennebury

Composition: MPS North America LLC

For permission to use material from this text or product,
submit all requests online at **cengage.com/permissions**
Further permissions questions can be emailed to
permissionrequest@cengage.com

Student Book with Online Workbook:
ISBN-13: 978-0-357-12471-0

Student Book:
ISBN-13: 978-0-357-11627-2

National Geographic Learning
20 Channel Center Street
Boston, MA 02210
USA

Locate your local office at **international.cengage.com/region**

Visit National Geographic Learning online at **ELTNGL.com**
Visit our corporate website at **www.cengage.com**

Printed in China
Print Number: 01 Print Year: 2019

CONTENTS

SCOPE AND SEQUENCE

ACADEMIC SKILLS

READING SKILL	VOCABULARY BUILDING	CRITICAL THINKING
A: Analyzing Infographics (1) B: Scanning for Specific Information	A: Prefix *uni-* B: Suffix *-ology*	A: Evaluating Evidence B: Evaluating Reasons
A: Analyzing a Writer's Claims B: Summarizing the Main Idea of Paragraphs	A: Word root *form* B: Collocations with *permanent*	A: Evaluating Claims B: Applying Ideas
A: Determining the Meaning of Unfamiliar Words B: Annotating a Reading Passage	A: Collocations with *physical* B: Words acting as nouns and verbs	A: Evaluating Problems B: Evaluating; Synthesizing
A: Summarizing a Text B: Analyzing Infographics (2)	A: Prefix *ex-* B: Collocations with *schedule*	A: Analyzing Pros and Cons B: Evaluating Visual Information; Justifying an Opinion
A: Summarizing Details on a Map B: Identifying a Writer's Point of View	A: Word web *spectacular* B: Collocations with *state*	A: Evaluating Ideas B: Inferring Opinions; Evaluating Using Criteria
A: Identifying Pros and Cons (1) B: Understanding Transitions	A: Word web *furthermore* B: Word root *vis*	A: Evaluating Pros and Cons B: Applying Ideas; Evaluating Pros and Cons
A: Identifying Pros and Cons (2) B: Identifying an Author's Opinion	A: Collocations with *steep* B: Word forms: verb, noun, adjective	A: Evaluating Pros and Cons B: Applying Ideas; Synthesizing
A: Understanding Vocabulary: Compound Words B: Inferring Information (1)	A: Word root *nov* B: Collocations with *dense*	A: Interpreting Meaning B: Synthesizing Ideas; Applying Ideas
A: Applying Information from a Text B: Recognizing Text Coherence	A: Word root *down* B: Collocations with *aid*	A: Evaluating Pros and Cons B: Applying Ideas; Evaluating Pros and Cons
A: Identifying Text Organization B: Recognizing Lexical Cohesion (1)	A: Collocations with *vast* B: Word root *nounce*	A: Applying Concepts B: Evaluating Using Criteria; Synthesizing Ideas
A: Inferring Information (2) B: Recognizing Lexical Cohesion (2)	A: Word root *sen(s)* B: Word root *nat*	B: Evaluating Evidence; Evaluating Pros and Cons; Synthesizing
A: Understanding Vocabulary: Phrasal Verbs B: Understanding Appositives	A: Prefix *-ize* B: Collocations with *precious*	A: Evaluating Challenges B: Speculating; Synthesizing

READING EXPLORER brings the world to your classroom.

With *Reading Explorer* you learn about real people and places, experience the world, and explore topics that matter.

What you'll see in the Third Edition:

Real-world stories give you a better understanding of the world and your place in it.

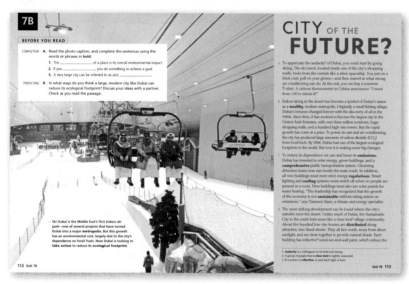

National Geographic Videos expand on the unit topic and give you a chance to apply your language skills.

Reading Skill and **Reading Comprehension** sections provide the tools you need to become an effective reader.

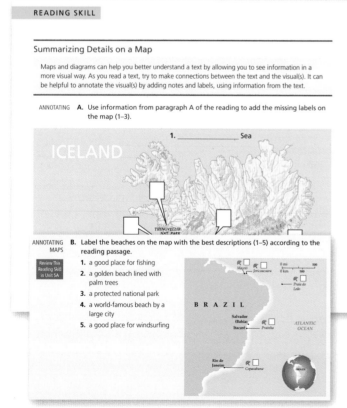

CRITICAL THINKING Evaluating Using Criteria In 1994, Ha Long Bay was recognized as a UNESCO World Heritage Site. There are two main categories of Heritage Sites: Natural and Cultural. To be included on UNESCO's Natural Heritage list, a site must have one of the following:

– unique natural phenomena   – exceptional natural beauty
– important wildlife habitats   – outstanding natural landforms

▶ Find out if there are any natural places in your country/region on UNESCO's list.
▶ Discuss in a small group: Are there any other natural places in your country/region that UNESCO should include? Note your ideas and share your reasons with another group.

Expanded Vocabulary Practice sections teach you the most useful words and phrases needed for academic reading.

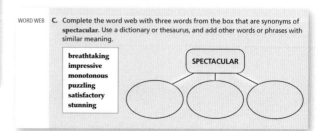

SPORTS AND FITNESS

A visually impaired
skier practices in a wind
tunnel to prepare for the
Paralympic Games.

WARM UP

Discuss these questions
with a partner.

1. What sports are popular
   in your country? Why
   are they popular?

2. Which types of athletes
   do you think are the
   fittest?

BEFORE YOU READ

PREVIEWING **A.** How much do you know about soccer? Read the sentences (1–4) and choose
T (true) or **F** (false). Then check your ideas when you read the passage.

1. The origins of soccer are more than 4,000 years old.   **T   F**

2. The modern sport of soccer started in Italy.   **T   F**

3. Globally, more than 200 million people play soccer.   **T   F**

4. Soccer is the most popular sport in Africa.   **T   F**

PREDICTING **B.** Why is soccer such a popular sport? Note your ideas. Then read the passage
and underline the reasons that are mentioned.

A soccer game on Mboro
Plage beach, Senegal

THE WORLD'S GAME

A Throughout history, humans have played some kind of kicking game. What the world now calls football—or soccer in the United States—began as far back as 2500 B.C.E. with the Chinese game of *cuju*. However, the sport we know today originated in Britain. In the 1840s, England's Football Association **established** a set of rules, and the modern game was born. Today, more than 200 million players all over the globe participate in the game, truly making soccer the world's sport.

B So, why is soccer so popular? Maybe it's the game's camaraderie:[1] the feeling that the team on the field is *your* team; their win is *your* **victory**, and their loss is *your* **defeat**. Or maybe it's the game's international quality. In countries like France, England, Spain, and Brazil, major teams have players from many different nations, and these clubs now have fans all over the world. Or perhaps it's the promise of great wealth. A number of professional soccer players, including Brazil's Neymar and Nigeria's Victor Moses, come from poor families. Today, both of these players make millions of euros every year.

C Soccer is popular for all of these reasons, but ultimately, the main reason for its **universal** appeal may be this: It's a simple game. It can be played anywhere with anything—a ball, a can, or even some bags tied together. And anyone can play it. "You don't need to be rich . . . to play soccer," says historian Peter Alegi. "You just need a flat space and a ball."

D It is this **unique** simplicity that makes soccer the most popular sport in Africa. Here, even in rural areas far from the bright lights and big stadiums, children and adults play the game, often with handmade balls.

---

1 **Camaraderie** is a feeling of friendship or team spirit among people who share an experience together.

A Love for Soccer

E The story of soccer in Africa is a long one. In the 19th century, European colonists[2] brought the game to Africa. Early matches were first played in the South African cities of Cape Town and Port Elizabeth in 1862. In time, the sport spread across the continent. Today, several of the game's best players come from African nations, including Senegal, Ivory Coast, Ghana, and Nigeria. All over the continent, thousands of soccer academies now **recruit** boys from poorer cities and towns to play the game. Many learn to play in their bare feet,[3] and they are tough, creative **competitors**. Their dream is to play for the national team or to join one of the big clubs in Europe someday. For some, the dream comes true.

F But the chance to make money with a professional team is probably not the main reason for soccer's popularity in Africa. "Soccer is the **passion** of everyone here," says Abubakari Abdul-Ganiyu, a teacher who works with youth clubs in Tamale, Ghana. "It unifies us." In fact, more than once, the game has helped to bring people together. In Ivory Coast, for example, immigrants[4] and Muslims faced discrimination[5] for years. Yet many of the country's best soccer players are from Muslim and immigrant families. As a result, the national team has become a symbol of **unity** and has helped to promote peace throughout the country.

G All over Africa, soccer is popular with parents and teachers for another reason: It keeps young people—especially boys—in school and out of trouble. "Most clubs in Tamale, Ghana, don't allow boys to play if they don't go to school," explains Abubakari. "We're trying our best to help young people and to make them **responsible** in society. Soccer helps us do this. For us, soccer is also a tool for hope."

---

2 **Colonists** are people who settle in a country which is ruled by another country.
3 If you do something **in your bare feet**, you do it without shoes.
4 An **immigrant** is a person who comes to live in a country from another country.
5 If you **face discrimination**, you experience unfair treatment because of your age, gender, etc.

Children in the Democratic Republic of the Congo play soccer with a ball made of string and tape.

SOCCER WITHOUT BORDERS

More than 200 national teams from six regions competed to get a place in 2018 FIFA World Cup in Russia. Thirty-two soccer teams qualified for the final tournament. Although each team represents a country, it doesn't mean all its players were born there. Family relations and dual citizenship (having two nationalities) influence which country a player plays for.

Of the 32 teams competing for the World Cup (shown here), 25 had at least one foreign-born player. In total, 97 foreign-born players competed in the 2018 World Cup.

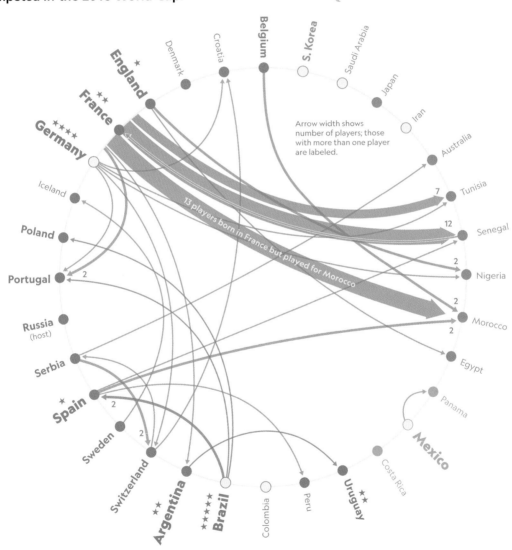

Arrow width shows number of players; those with more than one player are labeled.

13 players born in France but played for Morocco

Foreign-born player's connection from birthplace to World Cup team

National team with foreign-born players

National team with no foreign-born players

Not shown: 35 foreign-born players who were born in countries that didn't qualify

World Cup win

Country   15 or more appearances

Country   7–14 appearances

Country   6 or fewer appearances

A. Choose the best answer for each question.

GIST   **1.** What is this passage mainly about?

a. the history of soccer
b. the popularity of soccer
c. different soccer teams
d. how the World Cup began

DETAIL   **2.** In paragraph B, which of these is NOT given as a possible reason for soccer's popularity?

a. the team spirit among players and fans
b. famous players from different countries
c. the number of soccer games shown on TV
d. the possibility of making a lot of money

INFERENCE   **3.** What aspect of soccer is the author referring to by *It's a simple game* in paragraph C?

a. The rules are easy for people to understand.
b. You can play it anywhere with anything.
c. You don't need much talent to play soccer.
d. There are only a few versions of soccer.

REFERENCE   **4.** What does *some* refer to in the last line of paragraph E?

a. poor boys
b. cities and towns
c. soccer academies
d. national teams

MAIN IDEA   **5.** What is the main idea of the last paragraph?

a. More schools in Africa are opening soccer clubs.
b. Soccer helps people get better grades in school.
c. Older soccer players are passing on their skills to younger ones.
d. Soccer helps develop young people as members of society.

⌃ **Between 1930 and 2018, 79 national teams took part in a World Cup tournament.**

IDENTIFYING   **B. Match each statement (1–4) with the country it describes (a–e), according to the passage. One country is extra.**

| a. Britain | b. China | c. Ghana | d. Ivory Coast | e. South Africa |

1. _____ This is where the first games of soccer were played in Africa.

2. _____ A very early form of soccer was played here.

3. _____ This is where the soccer we know today originated.

4. _____ Some soccer clubs here allow boys to join only if they go to school.

Analyzing Infographics (1)

An infographic is a visual representation of information. It condenses a large amount of information into a combination of images, words, and numbers. Look for information in keys and captions, and other clues, such as the use of colors and lines, to help you understand how the parts of the infographic relate to each other.

ANALYZING INFOGRAPHICS

A. What information can you get from the "Soccer Without Borders" infographic? Check (✓) all that are true.

☐ a. how many teams with foreign-born players took part in the 2018 World Cup

☐ b. the number of foreign-born players in each team

☐ c. how far foreign-born players traveled to get to the World Cup

B. How does the infographic present its information? Match each feature (1–5) with the information it shows (a–e).

1. width of arrows •
2. direction of arrows •
3. size of country names •
4. color of country names •
5. the stars above country names •

• a. World Cups wins
• b. World Cup appearances
• c. regional confederation
• d. number of foreign-born players from one country
• e. player's country of birth to the country they play for

ANALYZING INFOGRAPHICS

C. Choose T (true) or F (false) for each statement about the infographic.

1. France has won the most World Cups.   **T**   **F**
2. South Korea has appeared in the World Cup finals more than six times.   **T**   **F**
3. Colombia had no foreign-born players in 2018.   **T**   **F**
4. Three players born in England played for Nigeria.   **T**   **F**

CRITICAL THINKING Evaluating Evidence   In paragraph A the writer states that soccer is "truly … the world's sport." What evidence is given to support the claim? Find and note two examples from the reading passage.

_____

_____

_____

COMPLETION **A.** Complete the information. Choose the correct words.

^ **In 2018, Ada Hegerberg became the first female winner of the "Golden Ball" world soccer award.**

In 2015, the Women's World Cup final attracted the biggest TV audience for a soccer game in U.S. history. But women's soccer wasn't always so popular. The big step forward came in 1991 when FIFA ¹**recruited / established** the Women's World Cup. In the final of that tournament, striker Michelle Anne Akers led the United States to ²**victory / unity** over Norway. Four years later, Norway ³**defeated / established** Germany in the final. Then, in 1996, ⁴**competitors / unity** from eight countries played in the first-ever women's soccer event at the Olympics. Since then, women's soccer has gone from strength to strength. Partly this is due to the popularity of world-class players like Marta from Brazil, Japan's Homare Sawa, and Ada Hegerberg from Norway. Top players with a ⁵**recruit / passion** for the sport are ⁶**universal / responsible** for helping make women's soccer hugely popular today.

DEFINITIONS **B.** Complete the sentences. Choose the correct options.

1. If you **recruit** someone to an organization, you want them to _____.
a. join   b. organize

2. Something that is **unique** is _____.
a. not as good as others   b. the only one of its kind

3. If something is **universal**, it relates to _____ in the world.
a. few people   b. all people

4. When there is **unity**, people _____.
a. act together   b. go separate ways

WORD LINK **C.** The prefix *uni-* in words such as **unity** means "one" or "single." Complete the sentences with the correct word from the box.

uniform   unite   unique   universal

1. In U.S. baseball, many teams have a home _____ that is mostly white.

2. A successful sports team can _____ a city or country.

3. Gaelic football is a sport _____ to Ireland.

4. Researchers believe the desire to play and be entertained is _____.

BEFORE YOU READ

COMPLETION   **A.** Read the photo caption below. Then complete sentences 1–3 using the words in **bold**.

1. Neymar, Serena Williams, and Lebron James are famous _____.
2. The world's biggest athletics _____ is the _____.
3. Winners of sporting events are often awarded _____.

PREDICTING   **B.** Read the title of the reading passage on the next page. List five factors in order of importance. Share your ideas with a partner.

⌄ **Athletes** from India, Spain, and Japan celebrate winning **medals** after the Women's Singles Badminton **competition** at the 2016 Rio Olympics.

WHAT MAKES AN OLYMPIC CHAMPION?

A How does a person become an Olympic **champion**—someone capable of winning the gold? In reality, a combination of biological, environmental, and **psychological** factors, as well as training and practice, all go into making a super athlete.

B Perhaps the most important factor involved in becoming an **elite** athlete is **genetic**. Most Olympic competitors are equipped with certain physical characteristics that **differentiate** them from the average person. Take an elite athlete's muscles, for example. In most human skeletal muscles (the ones that make your body move), there are fast-twitch fibers[1] and slow-twitch fibers. Fast-twitch fibers help us move quickly. Olympic weightlifters, for example, have a large number of fast-twitch fibers in their muscles— many more than the average person. These allow them to lift hundreds of kilos from the ground

and over their heads in seconds. Surprisingly, a large, muscular body is not the main **requirement** to do well in this sport. It is more important to have a large number of fast-twitch fibers in the muscles.

C The legs of an elite marathon runner, on the other hand, might contain up to 90 percent slow-twitch muscle fibers. These **generate** energy efficiently and enable an athlete to control fatigue and keep moving for a longer period of time. When we exercise long or hard, it's common to experience tiredness, muscle pain, and difficulty breathing. These feelings are caused when the muscles produce high amounts of a substance called lactate and can't remove it quickly enough. Athletes with many slow-twitch muscle fibers seem to be able to clear the lactate from their muscles faster as they move. Thus, the average runner might start

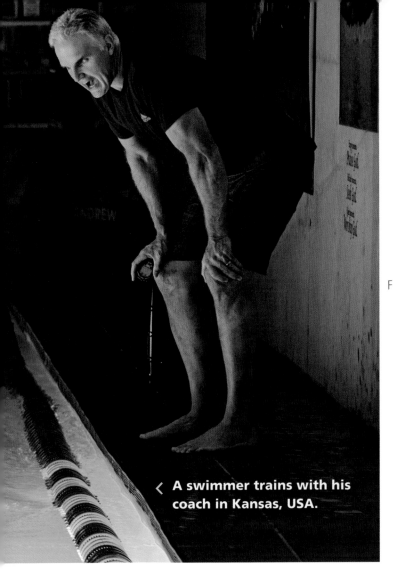

< **A swimmer trains with his coach in Kansas, USA.**

hemoglobin. Large amounts of hemoglobin carry oxygen around the body faster, enabling these athletes to run better. Cultural factors also help some athletes do well at certain sports. Tegla Loroupe, a young woman from northern Kenya, has won several marathons. She says some of her success is due to her country's altitude (she trains at about 2,400 meters) and some to her cultural background. As a child, she had to run 10 kilometers to school every day. "I'd be punished if I was late," she says.

F   Although genes, environment, and even culture play a part in becoming an elite athlete, training and practice are needed to succeed. Marathon runners may be able to control fatigue and keep moving for long periods of time, but they must train to reach and maintain their goals. Weightlifters and gymnasts perfect their skills by repeating the same motions again and again until they become **automatic**. Greg Louganis, winner of four Olympic diving gold medals, says divers must train the same way to be successful: "You have less than three seconds from takeoff until you hit the water, so it has to be reflex. You have to repeat the dives hundreds, maybe thousands, of times." Training this way requires an athlete to be not only physically fit but psychologically healthy as well. "They have to be," says Sean McCann, a sports psychologist at the Olympic Training Center in the United States. "Otherwise, they couldn't handle the training loads we put on them. [Athletes] have to be good at setting goals, generating energy when they need it, and managing anxiety."

G   How do athletes **adjust** to such intense pressure? Louganis explains how he learned to control his anxiety during a competition: "Most divers think too much . . . ," he says. "They're too much in their heads. What worked for me was humor. I remember thinking about what my mother would say if she saw me do a bad dive. She'd probably just compliment[2] me on the beautiful splash."

to feel discomfort halfway into a race. A trained Olympic athlete, however, might not feel pain until much later in the competition.

D   For some Olympic competitors, size is important. Most male champion swimmers are 180 cm or taller, allowing them to reach longer and swim faster. For both male and female gymnasts, though, a smaller size and body weight mean they can move with greater ease, and are less likely to suffer damage when landing on the floor from a height of up to 4.5 meters.

E   Some athletes' abilities are naturally **enhanced** by their environment. Those raised at high altitudes in countries such as Kenya, Ethiopia, and Morocco have blood that is rich in

---

1 Muscle **fibers** are thin, threadlike pieces of flesh that make up the muscles in your body.
2 If you **compliment** someone, you say something polite about their appearance or something they did.

A. Choose the best answer for each question.

GIST **1.** What is this reading mainly about?

    a. how to qualify for the Olympics

    b. factors that make someone a super athlete

    c. the different muscle types of a super athlete

    d. the size of a super athlete

INFERENCE **2.** Having a lot of slow-twitch muscle fibers is particularly important for _____.

    a. long-distance cyclists

    b. table-tennis players

    c. divers

    d. weightlifters

DETAIL **3.** When lactate builds up in their muscles, people feel _____.

    a. strength

    b. energy

    c. pain

    d. dizziness

∧ **The first Olympic medals were solid gold; however, the gold medals awarded at Rio 2016 were 92.5% silver.**

MAIN IDEA **4.** What is the main idea of paragraph F?

    a. Genes are an important part of athletic success.

    b. Marathon runners must train hard to succeed.

    c. Divers must train to be successful.

    d. Success in sports comes from a lot of practice.

INFERENCE **5.** What statement would diver Greg Louganis probably agree with?

    a. Athletes cannot perform well unless they are under pressure.

    b. It's important to practice and train hard, but not take things too seriously.

    c. A professional athlete should think carefully about each movement.

    d. It's important to joke with your teammates before you perform any sport.

CLASSIFYING **B. According to the passage, are the following especially important for marathon runners, gymnasts, or both? Add each one (a–f) to the Venn diagram.**

    a. training

    b. slow-twitch muscles

    c. practicing repeated motions

    d. small body size

    e. psychological health

    f. ability to control fatigue and keep moving for a long time

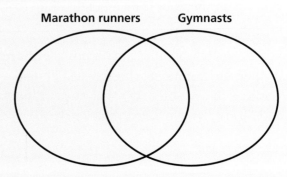

Marathon runners   **Gymnasts**

Scanning for Specific Information

The following tips can help you scan a text more effectively.

1. Decide what kind of information you need to scan for—a number, a person's name, or a specific word or phrase. For example, if you are scanning for the names of people or places, look for capitalized words.

2. Analyze the text before you scan. If the text is long, you may want to skim it first to determine where the information is likely to be.

3. Run your eyes over several lines of text at a time. When you find what you are searching for, read the entire sentence.

SCANNING **A.** For each item (1–5), decide what information you need to scan for (for example, a place or a name). Then scan the reading passage and write the correct information.

1. the height of most male champion swimmers _____

2. three countries with high altitudes _____

3. the chemical element that hemoglobin carries in our blood _____

4. the person who won four Olympic medals in diving _____

5. the place where sports psychologist Sean McCann works _____

SCANNING **B.** Read the statements (1–4). Then scan the passage and circle **T** (true) or **F** (false).

1. Genes are an important factor in becoming an elite athlete. **T** **F**

2. A marathon runner's legs can contain up to 90 percent slow-twitch muscle fibers. **T** **F**

3. Tegla Loroupe hasn't won a marathon. **T** **F**

4. Most dives take more than three seconds to complete. **T** **F**

CRITICAL THINKING Evaluating Effects The writer suggests that cultural factors affect how well someone does in sports. In what ways might the following factors have an effect on an athlete? Note your ideas and discuss with a partner.

| diet | education | family | gender roles | religion |

COMPLETION **A.** Complete the information with the correct form of the words from the box. Four words are extra.

adjust	automatic	champion	differentiate	elite
enhance	generate	genetic	psychological	require

In 2013, an ¹_____ swimmer named Diana Nyad became the first person to swim from Cuba to Florida without using a shark cage. Nyad had unsuccessfully attempted the 177-kilometer swim several times before, but at age 64, she finally completed it. The swim ²_____ Nyad to be in the water for nearly 53 hours. A 35-person team came with her, and (unlike her previous attempts) she wore a special suit and mask to keep jellyfish off her skin. Some suggested this equipment ³_____ her performance, though Nyad claimed it actually slowed her down.

What ⁴_____ this successful attempt from Nyad's four previous attempts? Importantly, the ⁵_____ she made to her equipment helped—she was previously stung many times by jellyfish. But experts believe the main difference was Nyad's mental determination, since her struggle was just as much ⁶_____ as physical. Her determination was so strong that even though she felt sick for much of the journey, she never gave up.

DEFINITIONS **B.** Match the definitions (1–5) to words from the box in **A**. Five words are extra.

1. the winner of a competition   _____

2. to produce or cause something to begin   _____

3. relating to your DNA   _____

4. to move or change something slightly   _____

5. happening without thought   _____

WORD LINK **C.** The suffix *-ology*, as in **psychology**, means "the study of." Add *-ology* to the word parts in the box to complete the definitions. One prefix is extra.

bi-	ge-	psych-	anthrop-

The study of …

1. human cultures _____

2. living things _____

3. physical structures of Earth _____

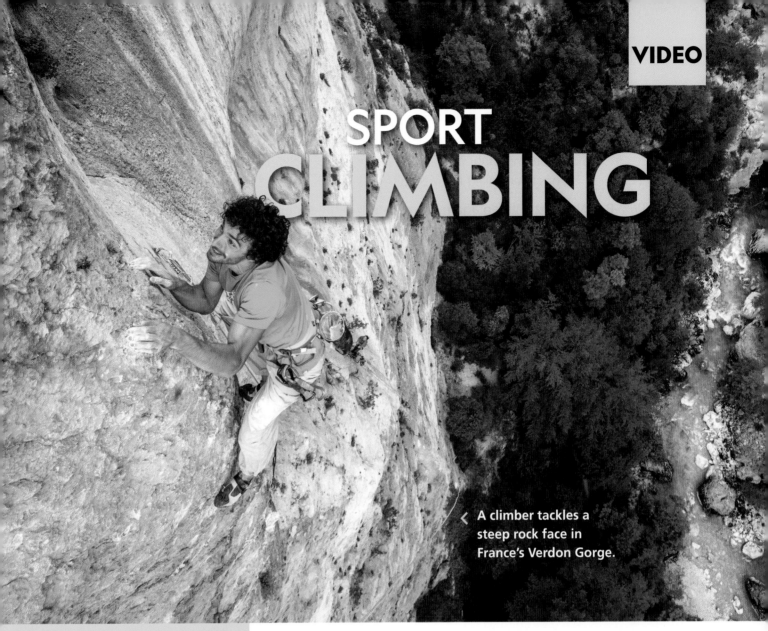

SPORT CLIMBING

< A climber tackles a steep rock face in France's Verdon Gorge.

BEFORE YOU WATCH

DEFINITIONS **A.** Read the information. The words in **bold** appear in the video. Match each word or phrase with its definition.

Sport climbing is a form of rock climbing. Whereas traditional rock climbers use removable hooks, or **anchors**, as they climb, sport climbers rely on using permanent anchors fixed to the rock. A popular place for sport climbing is Yosemite National Park in California, where climbers **push the limits** to set new routes and reach new heights. Less experienced sport climbers train on indoor climbing walls in a **gym** before going out onto a **rock face**. Now a popular global activity, sport climbing has also become an Olympic event, starting with the 2020 Summer Olympics in Tokyo.

1. **anchor** •   • a. to try to do something better than before

2. **push the limits** •   • b. an indoor place where people exercise

3. **gym** •   • c. a vertical surface area on a cliff or mountain

4. **rock face** •   • d. a device used in climbing for attaching a climber to a surface

GIST **A.** Watch the video. Which of the following is/are true about the Verdon Gorge, according to the video? Choose the best answer(s).

    a. It is has been a popular climbing destination for over a hundred years.

    b. It is an important place in the history of rock climbing.

    c. It has been called the Yosemite Valley of Europe.

COMPLETION **B.** Watch the video again. Complete the timeline of events in the history of Verdon. One item is extra.

a. large cracks	b. overhanging rocks	c. rock faces	d. training grounds

1960s   Verdon Gorge is thought to be impossible to climb.

1970s   Climbers start climbing Verdon using a few ¹_____ in the rock.

early 1980s   New technology enables climbers to move out onto flat ²_____.

mid-1980s   A challenging new route is created using ³_____.

CRITICAL THINKING Evaluating Reasons   Discuss answers to the questions with a partner.

▶ Consider sport climbing or another extreme sport. Why do you think people enjoy doing it? What are the main challenges and rewards?

_____

▶ What kind of personality traits do you think a rock climber needs? Why?

_____

VOCABULARY REVIEW

Do you remember the meanings of these words? Check (✓) the ones you know. Look back at the unit and review any words you're not sure of.

Reading A

☐ competitor	☐ defeat	☐ establish*	☐ passion	☐ recruit
☐ responsible	☐ unique*	☐ unity	☐ universal	☐ victory

Reading B

☐ adjust*	☐ automatic*	☐ champion	☐ differentiate*	☐ elite
☐ enhance*	☐ generate*	☐ genetic	☐ psychological*	☐ require*

* Academic Word List

SKIN DEEP

A Huli Wigman paints his face for a ceremony in Papua New Guinea.

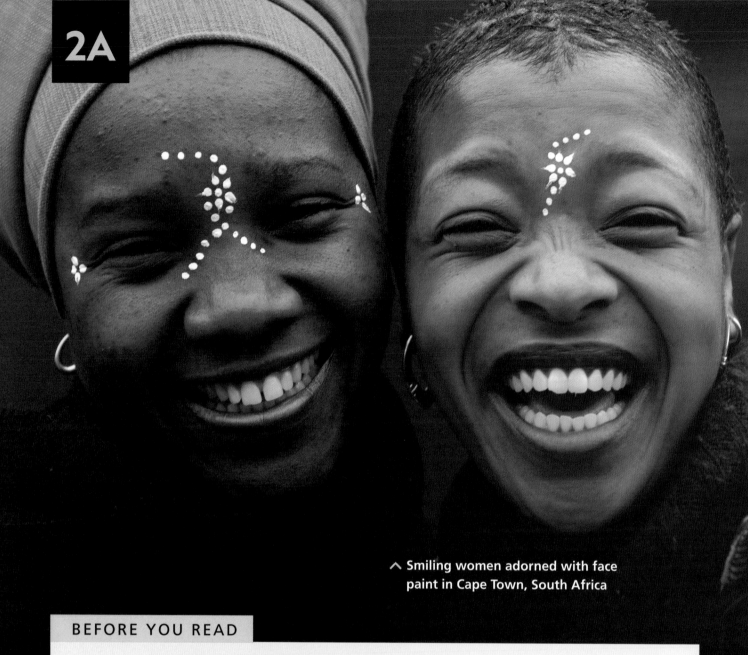

∧ **Smiling women adorned with face paint in Cape Town, South Africa**

BEFORE YOU READ

DISCUSSION **A.** Read the statements about beauty. Check (✓) the ones you agree with. Then discuss your answers with a partner.

☐ I spend a lot of time thinking about my appearance.

☐ I think good-looking people have easier lives than other people.

☐ I think it's fine for men to wear makeup.

☐ Women are judged on their looks more than men are.

PREVIEWING **B.** Work with a partner and note answers to these questions. Then read the passage and check your ideas.

1. Do you think people around the world probably have similar ideas about beauty and appearance? Why or why not?

2. In what ways do you think society and culture influence how we perceive, or regard, beauty?

WHAT IS BEAUTY?

A   The search for beauty spans centuries and continents. Paintings of Egyptians dating back over 4,000 years show both men and women painting their nails and wearing makeup. On the other side of the globe, the ancient Maya of Central America considered crossed eyes[1] beautiful, and hung little balls between children's eyes to develop this look. In 18th-century France, wealthy noblemen[2] wore large wigs of long white hair to make themselves attractive. In cultures throughout the world, people have gone to extreme lengths to achieve beauty.

B   Today, people continue to **devote** a lot of time and money to their appearance. According to a recent report, one out of three **consumers** globally say they are spending more money on beauty and health-care products than ever before. Worldwide, sales of makeup, dieting, hair- and skin-care products—as well as gym memberships and cosmetic surgery[3]—generate billions of dollars every year. And there is at least one good reason for the **desire** to be attractive: Beauty is power. Studies suggest that good-looking people make more money, get called on more often in class, and are perceived as friendlier.

C   But what exactly *is* beauty? Trying to define it is difficult, and yet we know it when we see it—or so we think. "Beauty is health," says one psychologist. "It's a billboard saying, 'I'm healthy. I can pass on your genes.'" And our awareness of it may start at a very early age. In one set of studies, six-month-old babies were shown a series of photographs. The faces in the pictures had been rated for attractiveness by a group of college students. In the studies, the babies spent more time looking at the attractive faces than the unattractive ones.

---

1 **Crossed eyes** are eyes that seem to look toward each other.
2 **Noblemen** are men who belong to a high rank, title, or status.
3 **Cosmetic surgery** is surgery done to make someone look more attractive.

> A Chinese opera star carefully applies her makeup.

D The idea that even babies judge appearance makes perfect sense to many researchers. In studies done by psychologists such as Victor Johnston at New Mexico State University and David Perrett at the University of St. Andrews in Scotland, men regularly showed a preference for women with certain **features**: larger eyes, clear skin, fuller lips, and a smaller nose and chin. Another study suggests that women prefer men with large shoulders and a narrow waist. According to scientists, the mind unconsciously tells men and women that these traits—the full lips, clear skin, strong shoulders—equal health and genetic well-being. In other words, it's a fundamental part of human nature to look for these qualities in a mate.

< **Actors in historical costumes prepare to perform a comedy by French playwright Molière.**

example, and the women on the pages are thin. But is this the "perfect" body type for women worldwide? Douglas Yu, a biologist from Great Britain, and Glenn Shepard, an anthropologist at the University of California at Berkeley, say no. For them, what is considered beautiful is **subjective** and varies around the world. Yu and Shepard found in one study, for example, that native peoples in southeast Peru preferred shapes regarded as overweight in Western cultures.

F Take another example: In every culture, one's hairstyle sends a clear message. In the Huli culture of Papua New Guinea, men grow their hair long as a symbol of health and strength. Teenage boys in this culture learn from a young age to style and decorate their hair—a behavior more commonly **associated with** the opposite **gender** in many cultures. It is also the men in this culture who are the objects of beauty. For certain festivals and celebrations, men dress up and paint their faces. The more colorful a man is, the more masculine[4]—and attractive—he is considered.

G For better or worse, beauty plays a role in our lives. But it is extremely difficult to define exactly what makes one person attractive to another. Although there do seem to be certain physical traits that are considered universally appealing, it is also true that beauty does not always **conform** to a single, **uniform** standard. In the end, beauty really is, as the saying goes, in the eye of the beholder.[5]

E Not everyone agrees with this **notion**, however. "Our hardwiredness can be altered by all sorts of expectations—predominantly cultural," says C. Loring Brace, an anthropologist at the University of Michigan. What is considered attractive in one culture might not be in another. Look in most Western fashion magazines, for

---

4 **Masculine** qualities and things are typical for men, as opposed to women.

5 If you **behold** something, you look at it.

A. Choose the best answer for each question.

GIST

1. What is this reading mainly about?

a. different ideas about beauty
b. the history of beauty
c. the world's most beautiful people
d. how beauty is power

DETAIL

2. The ancient Maya hung balls between children's eyes _____.

a. as a form of jewelry
b. to differentiate boys from girls
c. because they thought crossed eyes were beautiful
d. to add an attractive "third" eye

> A beauty treatment using snails is demonstrated at a salon in Tokyo.

DETAIL

3. In paragraph C, the babies in the study _____.

a. were shown photos of attractive students
b. were entered into a beauty contest
c. were rated for their beauty
d. were able to tell attractive from unattractive faces

VOCABULARY

4. In the second sentence of paragraph E, *predominantly* can be replaced with _____.

a. hardly
b. mainly
c. exactly
d. probably

DETAIL

5. What determines the beauty of a Huli man in Papua New Guinea?

a. how young he is
b. his colorful makeup
c. his strength
d. the size of his mask

SCANNING FOR INFORMATION

Review this reading skill in Unit 1B

B. Which paragraphs of the reading passage (A–F) contain the following information?

1. an argument that culture plays a part in perceptions of beauty _____

2. an explanation of how some standards of beauty might be universal _____

3. a definition of *beauty* _____

4. a reference to the beauty-care industry _____

5. an example of a culture where men wear makeup _____

6. a time frame _____

Analyzing a Writer's Claims

A reading passage may contain one or more claims—statements that suggest something is true or real—made by the writer. As a reader, it's important to evaluate these claims to see how well they are supported. There are several ways to support a claim.

Claim: In the United States, cosmetic surgery is increasingly popular.

- **Reason**: One reason for this is that certain cosmetic surgeries are becoming more affordable.
- **Example**: Several popular reality-TV shows depict the positive side of the industry.
- **Statistics**: According to the American Society of Plastic Surgeons, there were 17.5 million cosmetic procedures performed in 2017, a 2 percent increase from the year before.
- **Expert opinion**: According to the head surgeon of one leading clinic, more people are now looking for ways to reshape their bodies.

ANALYZING
CLAIMS

A. Look back at paragraphs A–C in the reading passage to complete these student notes.

> "The search for beauty spans centuries and continents." (paragraph A)
> - Egyptian 4,000 y. o. paintings show ppl w/ painted [1]_____
> - 18th c. French noblemen wore large white [2]_____
>
> "Today, people continue to devote a lot of time and money to their appearance." (paragraph B)
> - 1 out of [3]_____ people spending more money
> - [4]_____ of $$$ in sales of beauty products + services worldwide
>
> "[O]ur awareness of it may start at a very early age." (paragraph C)
> - [5]_____-month-old babies spent more time looking at attractive faces than unattractive ones

ANALYZING
CLAIMS

B. The writer makes claims that perceptions of beauty may or may not be universal. Note down how the writer supports these claims. _____

_____

CRITICAL THINKING Evaluating Claims

Discuss these questions with a partner.

▶ What do you think the expression "Beauty is in the eye of the beholder" (paragraph G) means?
  a. Beauty is perceived differently by different people.
  b. Without vision, we can't perceive beauty
  c. Beauty is held in very high regard.

▶ Can you think of some examples to support this opinion?

VOCABULARY PRACTICE

COMPLETION **A.** Complete the information using the correct form of the words or phrases in the box. One word is extra.

associate with	conform	consumer
devote	gender	notion

Anita Roddick (1942–2007)

Anita Roddick, founder of The Body Shop, was committed to improving the world we live in. Throughout her career she refused to [1]_____ to business practices that she saw as destructive to the environment. Roddick believed in the [2]_____ that "business can and must be a force for positive social change." These beliefs meant her company [3]_____ time and money to raising awareness of the need to protect the environment. She supported developing countries, and created more environmentally friendly beauty products for [4]_____ to buy. While Roddick is most closely [5]_____ The Body Shop, she also started a charity to help children in various parts of the world. Roddick died in 2007, but The Body Shop is still a model for ethically conscious businesses everywhere.

COMPLETION **B.** Complete the sentences using the correct form of the words in the box. One word is extra.

desire	feature	gender
notion	subjective	uniform

1. People don't have _____ ideas on what beauty is; opinions vary greatly.

2. Nowadays, many people of both _____ buy and use cosmetics.

3. People use makeup to enhance their _____—for example, by using blush to make their cheeks look pinker and healthier.

4. Our ideas about beauty are highly _____; what one person finds attractive may be unattractive to another.

5. The _____ to look young has led to a boom in sales of anti-aging products.

WORD LINK **C.** The word root *form*, as in **uniform**, means "shape." Complete the sentences with the correct form of the words in the box. One word is extra.

deformed	format	conform	transform	uniform

1. There isn't a _____ standard for indicating shoe size—a men's size 10 in the U.K is a size 9 in Mexico and a size 273 in Korean.

2. Students are expected to _____ to the rules and regulations written in the school handbook.

3. Volunteers _____ the old warehouse into an exciting art space.

4. Many colleges expect essays to be _____ in 12-point font.

BEFORE YOU READ

DISCUSSION **A.** Work with a partner. Brainstorm three ways that people can change the appearance of their skin.

PREVIEWING **B.** Why do you think people change their skin in these ways? Note some reasons. Then read the passage and check your answers.

> Facial and body tattoos are common among the Maori of New Zealand.

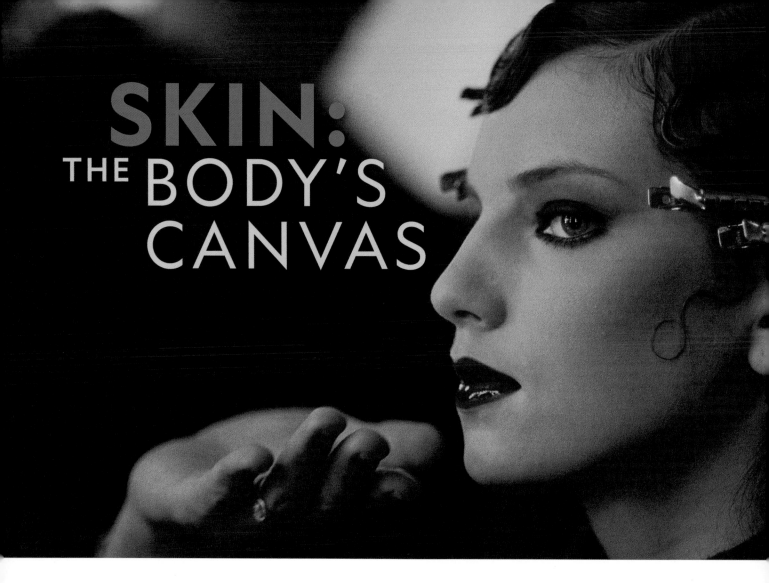

SKIN: THE BODY'S CANVAS

A If you could take off your skin and lay it flat, it would cover an area of about 1.9 square meters. Skin is, by far, the body's largest organ. Covering almost the entire body, skin protects us from a variety of **external** forces. For example, it protects us from extremes of temperature, damaging sunlight, harmful chemicals, and dangerous infections. Skin is also packed with nerves, which keeps the brain in touch with the outside world. The health of our skin and its ability to perform its **protective** functions are **crucial** to our well-being. However, the appearance of our skin is equally—if not more—important to many people on this planet.

B Take skin color, for example. Your genes determine your skin's color, but for centuries, humans have tried to lighten or darken their skin in an attempt to be more attractive. In the 1800s, white skin was desirable for many Europeans. Skin this color meant that its owner was a member of the upper class and did not have to work in the sun. Among darker-skinned people in some parts of the world, products used to lighten skin are still popular today. During the 20th century, attitudes toward light skin shifted in the opposite direction in other cultures, as cities grew and work moved indoors. Tanned skin began to indicate **leisure** time and health. In many places today, tanning on the beach or in a salon remains popular, even though people are more aware of the dangers of UV rays.[1]

Identity and Status

C Just as people have altered their skin's color to denote wealth and beauty, so too have cultures around the globe marked their skin to indicate

< A model prepares for Fashion Week in New York City.

wants to have. The process of getting a full-body tattoo is both slow and painful and can take two years or more to complete.

E In some cultures, scarring—a marking caused by cutting or burning the skin—is practiced, usually among people who have darker skin on which a tattoo would be difficult to see. For many men in West Africa, for instance, scarring is a rite of passage—an act that symbolizes that a male has **matured** from a child into an adult. In Australia, among some native peoples, cuts are made on the skin of both men and women when they reach age 16 or 17. Without these, they were traditionally not permitted to trade, sing ceremonial songs, or participate in other activities.

F Not all skin markings are **permanent**, though. In countries such as Morocco and India, women decorate their skin with colorful henna designs for celebrations such as weddings and important religious holidays. The henna coloring, which comes from a plant, **fades** and disappears over time.

G In recent years in many industrialized nations, tattooing, henna body art, and, to a lesser degree, scarring have been gaining in popularity. What makes these practices appealing to those living in modern cities? According to photographer Chris Rainier, whose book *Ancient Marks* examines body markings around the globe, people are looking for a connection with the traditional world. "There is a whole **sector** of modern society—people in search of identity, people in search of meaning . . .," says Rainier. "Hence, [there has been] a huge explosion of tattooing and body marking." Rainier reasons that it's "mankind wanting identity, wanting a sense of place . . . and a sense of culture within their community."

cultural identity or community **status**. Tattooing, for example, has been carried out for thousands of years. Leaders in places including ancient Egypt, Britain, and Peru wore tattoos to mark their status, or their bravery. Today, among the Maori people of New Zealand as well as in cultures in Samoa, Tahiti, and Borneo, full-facial tattoos are still used to identify the wearer as a member of a certain family. These tattoos can also symbolize the person's achievements in life.

D In Japan, tattooing has been practiced for thousands of years, but was outlawed in the 19th century. Although there are no laws against it today, tattoos are still strongly associated with **criminals**—particularly the *yakuza*, or the Japanese mafia,[2] who are known for their full-body tattoos. The complex design of a *yakuza* member's tattoo usually includes symbols of character traits that the wearer

---

1 **UV rays** (or **ultraviolet rays**) from sunlight cause your skin to become darker.
2 The **mafia** commonly refers to a criminal organization that makes money illegally.

A. Choose the best answer for each question.

GIST

1. What is this reading mainly about?

a. the skin's role in our overall health
b. the ways people change the appearance of their skin
c. the different reasons people get tattoos
d. cultural ceremonies that involve skin tattooing

INFERENCE

2. What can we infer about the tattoos of the Maori?

a. Only men get facial tattoos.
b. Members of the same family have similar facial tattoos.
c. No one gets their entire face tattooed anymore.
d. Both men and women get facial tattoos but never body tattoos.

DETAIL

3. Why are tattoos disapproved of in Japanese society?

a. They are often associated with crime.
b. They often have political messages.
c. They look unattractive.
d. They can only be made illegally.

REFERENCE

4. In the last sentence of paragraph E, what does *these* refer to?

a. cuts   c. males
b. customs   d. celebrations

The scars on the face of a Gobir woman from Niger indicate her tribal membership.

DETAIL

5. What is NOT true about henna designs?

a. They are used to celebrate religious holidays.
b. Women decorate their skin with them.
c. They are permanent.
d. They are made with plants.

ANALYZING CLAIMS

Review this reading skill in Unit 2A

B. Write short answers to the questions below. Use up to three words or numbers from the passage for each answer.

1. Skin is "… by far the body's largest organ." How big is it, exactly?

_____

2. Skin "protects us from a variety of external forces." What is ONE example of an external force?

_____

3. "In recent years in many industrialized nations, tattooing … [has] been gaining in popularity." What is the name of the expert who gives an opinion about this?

_____

Summarizing the Main Idea of Paragraphs

Understanding the main idea of each paragraph can be especially useful when taking notes, or when creating a summary outline or word web of the reading. As you read, one strategy is to summarize the main idea of each paragraph so that you can easily identify it later. For each paragraph, read the first sentence and then quickly skim the rest of the paragraph. Then determine what the paragraph is mainly about and write a short note in the margin.

SUMMARIZING
THE MAIN IDEA

A. Look back at the reading passage. Choose the main idea of paragraphs A–C.

1. Paragraph A

a. the role our skin plays in our overall health
b. the importance of skin health and appearance

2. Paragraph B

a. the reasons for changing skin color in recent centuries
b. skin tanning as a symbol of leisure time and health

3. Paragraph C

a. the history of facial tattooing   b. cultural reasons for tattooing

B. Now identify and note the main idea of paragraphs D–F.

Paragraph D _____

_____

Paragraph E _____

_____

Paragraph F _____

_____

CRITICAL THINKING Applying Ideas

▶ What do people do to express their individual identity? Add more items to the list below.

Get tattoo of important cultural symbols (e.g., an angel)
Dye hair a different color (e.g., pink)

_____

_____

_____

▶ Which of the things above have you done? Which would you consider doing? Why or why not?

VOCABULARY PRACTICE

COMPLETION **A.** Complete the information using the words in the box. Three words are extra.

∧ **A tattooed member of the Iban tribe**

criminal	**crucial**	**external**	**fade**
mature	**permanent**	**protective**	**sector**

Tattooing was traditionally a(n) ¹_____ part of life for members of the Iban tribe of Sarawak, Malaysia. Iban tattooing was a spiritual art form. It was believed to have ²_____ powers—defending the Iban people from harm and disease. Originally, the tattooing was done using ancient recipes involving natural dyes from plants, and traditional wooden tools. The dyes were ³_____ and could not be removed. Newly done Iban tattoos look dark, but they gradually ⁴_____ somewhat from sunlight, or as the dye is absorbed into the skin. Today, for a growing ⁵_____ of Iban society, Western tattoos are more popular than traditional designs. Modern chemical dyes have mainly replaced the plant-based ones.

DEFINITIONS **B.** Complete the sentences. Choose the correct words.

1. A **criminal** is a person who _____ the law.
   a. follows   b. breaks

2. A **leisure** activity is one you enjoy doing when you _____ working.
   a. are   b. are not

3. Something **external** is on the _____.
   a. inside, not the outside   b. outside, not the inside

4. You are more likely to describe a _____ as **mature**.
   a. two-year-old   b. 30-year-old

5. A person's **status** relates to their _____ in society.
   a. rank or position   b. health and diet

COLLOCATIONS **C.** The nouns in the box are frequently used with the adjective **permanent**. Complete the sentences with the correct words. One word is extra.

address	**basis**	**damage**	**housing**	**resident**

1. Excessive sunburn can cause permanent _____ to your skin.

2. It's helpful to have a permanent _____ to receive your mail.

3. For foreign-born nationals, it can take many years to become a permanent _____ of Australia.

4. Many part-time workers hope to get hired on a permanent _____.

THE BEAUTY OF UGLY FOOD

BEFORE YOU WATCH

DEFINITIONS
A. The words and phrases in **bold** appear in the video. Circle the best word or phrase to complete each definition.

Do you ever buy food based on how it looks? Many kinds of **produce** are judged on unrealistic standards of beauty. In fact, experts estimate that about a third of the planet's fruits and vegetables goes to waste due to strict **cosmetic** standards. Supermarkets and other **retailers** often sell only produce that meets certain size, shape, and color **specifications**. Items that are seen as **below grade**—including ones that are slightly damaged or **bruised**—are **rejected** and do not make it onto the shelves.

1. If you describe something as **cosmetic**, you are describing its *appearance / meaning*.
2. The **produce** section of a supermarket sells *fruit and vegetables / meat and fish*.
3. A food **retailer** is a company that sells food to *customers / other businesses.*
4. If someone **rejects** something, they *demand / refuse* to have it.
5. If a fruit is **bruised**, it has a *mark on it / strange shape*.

PREVIEWING
B. Are there particular fruits or vegetables that you won't buy if the size, shape, or color looks wrong? Discuss with a partner.

VIEWING **A.** Watch the video. Then choose the best answer.

This video is mostly about _____.

    a. efforts to change perceptions of "ugly" food
    b. several examples of innovative supermarkets in California
    c. the rising demand for more "beautiful" produce

MULTIPLE CHOICE **B.** Watch the video again. Then choose the best option for each question or statement.

1. According to the video, what happens to California pears that are bruised?

    a. They are thrown away.   b. They are canned and juiced.

2. In the video, what makes Chuck Baker sad?

    a. the thought that his pears are getting thrown away
    b. the overall decline in the U.S. pear market

3. When Ron Clark says, "It's up to us to put pressure on the retailers," he means that _____.

    a. If people want to buy "ugly" fruit, they have to go straight to the farms.
    b. If people want stores to sell "ugly" fruit, they have to tell the stores.

4. According to the video, Ron Clark's company is trying to _____.

    a. show people that "ugly" fruit is actually healthier than other fruit.
    b. get "ugly" fruit into stores so people can buy it

CRITICAL THINKING Applying Ideas   Discuss your answers to the questions with a partner.

▶ Would you shop at a store that only sells imperfect produce? Why or why not?

▶ What might be some other ways to reduce the amount of "ugly food" that goes to waste?

VOCABULARY REVIEW

Do you remember the meanings of these words? Check (✓) the ones you know. Look back at the unit and review any words you're not sure of.

Reading A

☐ associate with   ☐ conform*   ☐ consumer*   ☐ desire   ☐ devote*

☐ feature   ☐ gender   ☐ notion*   ☐ subjective   ☐ uniform*

Reading B

☐ criminal   ☐ crucial*   ☐ external*   ☐ fade   ☐ leisure

☐ mature*   ☐ permanent   ☐ protective   ☐ sector*   ☐ status*

* Academic Word List

ANIMALS IN DANGER

3

WARM UP

Discuss these questions with a partner.

1. What animals can you think of that are in danger?

2. What are some reasons that animals become endangered?

∧ A 24-day-old Bengal slow loris at the Endangered Primate Rescue Center, Vietnam

BEFORE YOU READ

PREVIEWING **A.** How much do you know about koalas? Read each sentence (1–3) and circle the answer.

1. A koala's diet consists mainly of **tree nuts / tree leaves**.

2. Baby koalas live for several months **with their father / in their mother's pouch**.[1]

3. There used to be 10 million koalas in the wild. Today, there are about **80,000 / 800,000** koalas left in the wild.

PREDICTING **B.** Read the title and headings in the passage. Why do you think koalas are at risk? List some possible reasons. Check your ideas as you read the passage.

_____

_____

1 A **pouch** is a pocket-like place

Caregiver Anika Lehmann looks after a koala named Talisa before releasing her back into the wild.

RACING TO RESCUE KOALAS

A It's two in the morning, and a koala is caught on a fence, like a prisoner trying to escape. A phone rings in the home of Megan Aitken in a **suburb** of Brisbane, on the east coast of Australia. Aitken runs a volunteer organization devoted to rescuing wild koalas. Before she is told the location, she has already thrown her clothes over her pajamas, ready to head out.

B When Aitken arrives on the scene, two other volunteers—Jane Davies and Sandra Peachey—are already there. They discover that the koala's fur is caught in the barbed wire.[1] Nearby, they notice tall eucalyptus trees. "He was obviously trying to get to the trees on the other side," Aitken says.

C Aitken puts on heavy gloves. Despite their cute appearance, koalas can be ferocious when resisting **capture**. If they feel **threatened**, they bite, and Aitken has the scars to prove it. The volunteers get to work. Davies throws a blanket over the animal, while Peachey opens the lid of a cage. Aitken firmly **grasps** the koala through the blanket, frees it from the fence, and drops it in the cage.

D Next, they check the animal's **physical** condition. If the koala is sick or injured, it may need to be taken to an animal hospital. If the koala is healthy—like this one—it is normally released where it is found. Koalas **tend to** live in a small area, and often eat from the same trees over and over.

E Right now, however, Aitken and the rescued koala are in a suburb with almost no trees. "This is the whole problem," Aitken says. "There are so few places left for the koala." In the end, Aitken takes the animal to a small park nearby and releases him. "Good luck, little one," she says.

Koalas at Risk

F "Koalas are getting caught in fences and dying," explains Deidré de Villiers, a koala researcher in Queensland, Australia. Others are being killed by dogs or struck by vehicles, she says. Some even die "simply because a homeowner cut down several eucalyptus trees in his backyard."

G For 15 years, de Villiers has been studying koalas and the reasons for their disappearance. She is also working on ways to make suburban areas more koala-friendly. De Villiers believes that koalas and humans can live together, if certain changes are made. She recommends reducing speed limits on streets and creating more green areas for koalas to live in. Even more important is the need to preserve eucalyptus trees.

---

1 **Barbed wire** has sharp pieces of metal attached to it; it is often used to make fences.

H Even if these changes are made, koalas still have another problem. "Disease is a huge issue," explains veterinarian[2] Jon Hanger. Hanger says that almost half of Queensland's female koalas are affected by a disease called *chlamydiosis*. Without treatment, the koalas are unable to **reproduce**. "Koala populations that used to be vibrant are becoming **extinct**," says Hanger. Once, there were millions of koalas in Australia; now, there are believed to be fewer than 80,000.

A Friend to Koalas

I At her home near Brisbane, Deidré de Villiers is taking care of a female koala named Ruby. "Ruby still sleeps in the basket hugging her teddy bear," she says. "She was rescued from the jaws of a dog." Every two days, de Villiers collects eucalyptus leaves, the koala's **primary** food, from a nearby farm to feed Ruby. For 12 years, she has cared for more than 60 koalas.

---

2 A **veterinarian** is an animal doctor.

LOSING THEIR EUCALYPTUS

Over two centuries ago, about ten million koalas lived in forests on the east coast of Australia. Eucalyptus leaves—their primary food source—were plentiful. By the start of this century, nearly two-thirds of the forests had been cleared, leaving fewer than 80,000 koalas left in the wild.

1750

☐ Approximate koala distribution

▨ Potential koala habitat

0 mi   200

0 km   200

2001

QUEENSLAND

Lake Samsonvale • Beerwah
⊙ Brisbane
Koala Coast

SOUTH AUSTRALIA

NEW SOUTH WALES

★ Canberra, A.C.T.

VICTORIA

J Later, de Villiers visits a forest near Brisbane to catch Tee Vee, a wild female koala. De Villiers has been following Tee Vee for over a year. Using special audio equipment, de Villiers walks and listens for a **signal** from the koala's radio collar.[3] She eventually finds Tee Vee sitting on a tree branch 15 meters high. As de Villiers climbs up a ladder, Tee Vee starts moving down the tree. Then, suddenly, the koala jumps into the air and lands on the ground. She is quickly captured by de Villiers's team.

K Tee Vee is given medicine to relax her. Next, de Villiers measures the length of the koala's body and head. She also checks Tee Vee's teeth and the condition of her fur. "I think she has a baby," de Villiers says. She carefully opens the koala's pouch and takes out a 10-centimeter-long baby koala. De Villiers examines the baby for any problems. Then she puts it back in the mother's pouch. "As long as there are healthy babies," she says, "there's still hope."

---

3 A **collar** is something an animal wears around its neck.

The "little guys are part of our family," says Samantha Longman, who is raising four orphan koalas.

A. Choose the best answer for each question.

GIST   **1.** What is this reading mainly about?

   a. how one woman is saving koalas from extinction
   b. ways that humans and koalas can learn to live together
   c. new methods for studying koalas in the wild
   d. threats to koalas and efforts to protect them

DETAIL   **2.** What does Megan Aitken use the blanket for?

   a. to catch the koala after it falls from a tree
   b. to cover the koala so it doesn't harm her
   c. to keep the koala warm after it's placed in the cage
   d. to place over the cage so the koala inside stays calm

INFERENCE   **3.** Why is the koala that Aitken caught released in a nearby park?

   a. because koalas feed in the same trees again and again
   b. because it's the only place nearby that has eucalyptus trees
   c. because that's where the koala probably has its baby
   d. because wild koalas are not allowed in residential areas

> **A koala recovers from an arm injury after being struck by a car.**

DETAIL   **4.** According to Deidré de Villiers, what is the main thing that suburban areas must do to protect koalas?

   a. lower speed limits in areas with koalas
   b. build green corridors for koala movement
   c. preserve koalas' existing eucalyptus trees
   d. create special koala-only habitat zones

INFERENCE   **5.** Why do you think de Villiers captures Tee Vee?

   a. to see if she had her baby
   b. to attach a signaling device to her
   c. to check on her condition
   d. to take her to an animal hospital

MAIN IDEAS   **B.** Match each paragraph from the reading to its main idea. One idea is extra.

1. Paragraph C _____   a. ways to help protect koalas

2. Paragraph D _____   b. the need to protect oneself from koalas

3. Paragraph F _____   c. how a researcher checks the health of a koala

4. Paragraph G _____   d. examples of how koalas are being killed

5. Paragraph K _____   e. what to do when a koala is sick, or is healthy

   f. the environmental benefits of koalas

Determining the Meaning of Unfamiliar Words

When you come across an unfamiliar word, use these strategies to understand its meaning:

1. Look at the word's prefixes (e.g., *pre-, re-, un-*) and suffixes (e.g., *-tion, -able, -ology*).

2. Guess the word's meaning by looking at the context—the words, sentences, and ideas around it.

3. Look for synonyms or antonyms of the word used elsewhere in the paragraph.

4. Determine the word's part of speech and use a dictionary to check its meaning. Be sure you check the definition with the original sentence as some words have more than one meaning, even for one part of speech.

ANALYZING **A.** Look back at the reading passage. Find and underline the words in **bold** below. Then use the strategies above to choose the best meaning.

1. obviously (paragraph B)

    a. clearly   b. slowly   c. strangely

2. ferocious (paragraph C)

    a. calm   b. stupid   c. violent

3. released (paragraph D)

    a. set free   b. cleaned up   c. given food

4. treatment (paragraph H)

    a. a partner   b. being left alone   c. medical assistance

5. vibrant (paragraph H)

    a. unknown   b. kept in zoos   c. healthy and numerous

ANALYZING **B.** Find three more unfamiliar words in the reading passage. Note them below. Use the strategies above to determine the meaning of the words. Then use a dictionary to check your answers.

CRITICAL THINKING Evaluating Problems

▶ What are the two main threats facing koalas discussed in the reading passage? Note down your answer below.

▶ Which of these threats do you think is easier to solve? Why? Discuss your ideas with a partner.

COMPLETION **A. Complete the information. Circle the correct words.**

Large and flightless, the cassowary lives in the rain forests of northern Australia. In recent years, human activity has driven the cassowary nearly to ¹**reproduction / extinction**. They ²**tend to / grasp** shy away from people, but are seen occasionally in city ³**capture / suburbs**. There they get hit by cars and sometimes attacked by dogs. The birds even fall into traps meant to ⁴**capture / signal** wild pigs. But it is land development that really ⁵**threatens / grasps** cassowaries. Large areas of forest in northern Queensland have been cut down, which has had a devastating effect on their numbers. Roads carve up the forest, so their ⁶**signal / primary** habitat is no longer a single area. This makes it hard for young cassowaries to find their own territories. Local people have begun replanting fields and linking rain forest sections so cassowaries don't have to cross roads.

∧ **At almost 60 kg, the northern cassowary is one of the world's heaviest birds.**

DEFINITIONS **B. Complete the sentences. Choose the correct words.**

1. When you **grasp** something with your hand, you hold it _____.
   a. loosely
   b. tightly

2. Your **physical** condition relates to your _____.
   a. mind
   b. body

3. An example of a **signal** might be _____.
   a. a deep thought
   b. a flashing light

4. Two animals that **reproduce** _____.
   a. have a baby
   b. fight each other

COLLOCATIONS **C. The nouns in the box are often used with physical. Add them to the correct sentences. One word is extra.**

| appearance | condition | contact | education | exercise |

1. The most distinctive aspect of a toucan's _____ is its huge orange beak.
2. Physical _____, such as walking, is important to keep fit and healthy.
3. After an oil spill, many seabirds are in poor physical _____.
4. As is the case with most wild animals, humans should avoid physical _____ with koalas.

BEFORE YOU READ

DISCUSSION **A.** Read the photo caption below. Then discuss your answers to these questions with a partner.

    1. What kinds of challenges do you think a snow leopard faces?

    2. In what ways do you think it has adapted to its environment?

PREDICTING **B.** Read the title and the headings in the reading passage. Check (✓) the information that you think the passage will include. Then read and check your ideas.

    ☐ the number of snow leopards left in the wild

    ☐ methods of protecting snow leopards

    ☐ how young snow leopards survive in the wild

    ☐ disagreements between snow leopards and herders

‹ Snow leopards live at elevations between 3,000 and 5,000 meters in the mountains of Central Asia.

TRACKING THE SNOW LEOPARD

A   "When a snow leopard stalks its prey among the mountain walls, it moves . . . softly, slowly," explains Indian biologist Raghunandan Singh Chundawat, who has studied the animal for years. "If it knocks a stone loose, it will reach out a foot to stop it from falling and making noise." One might be moving right now, perfectly silent, maybe close by. But where?

B   Best known for its spotted coat and long **distinctive** tail, the snow leopard is one of the world's most secretive animals. These elusive[1] cats can only be found high in the remote, mountainous regions of Central Asia. For this reason, and because they hunt primarily at night, they are very rarely seen.

C   Snow leopards have been **officially** protected since 1975, but **enforcing** this law has proven difficult. Many continue to be killed for their fur and body parts, which are worth a fortune on the black market.[2] In recent years, though, **conflict** with local herders has also led to a number of snow leopard deaths. This is because the big cats kill the herders' animals, and **drag** the bodies away high up in the mountains to eat.

< When hunting, snow leopards have been known to leap more than nine meters, six times their body length.

D As a result of these pressures, the current snow leopard population is estimated at only 4,000 to 7,000, and some fear that the actual number may already have dropped below 3,500. The only way to **reverse** this trend and bring these cats back from their threatened **status**, say conservationists, is to make them more valuable alive than dead.

A Fragile Relationship

E Because farming is difficult in Central Asia's cold, dry **landscape**, traditional cultures depend mostly on livestock (mainly sheep and goats) to survive in these mountainous regions. At night, when snow leopards hunt, herders' animals are in danger of snow leopard attacks. If a family loses even a few animals, it can push them into desperate **poverty**. "The wolf comes and kills, eats, and goes somewhere else," said one herder, "but snow leopards are always around. They have killed one or two animals many times . . . Everybody wanted to finish this leopard."

---

1 Something that is **elusive** is difficult to find.
2 If something is bought or sold on the **black market**, it is done illegally.

F To address this problem, local religious leaders have called for an end to snow leopard killings, saying that these wild animals have the right to exist peacefully. They've also tried to convince people that the leopards are quite rare, and thus it is important to protect them.

The Value of Preservation

G Financial incentives are also helping to slow snow leopard killings. The organization Snow Leopard Conservancy India Trust has established Himalayan Homestays, a program that sends visitors to herders' houses. For a clean room and bed, meals with the family, and an introduction to their culture, visitors pay about ten U.S. dollars a night. If guests come once every two weeks through the tourist season, the herders will earn enough income to replace the animals lost to snow leopards. In addition, the organization helps herders build protective fences that keep out snow leopards. It also conducts environmental classes at village schools, and trains the organization's members as nature guides, available for hire. In exchange, the herders agree not to kill snow leopards.

H In Mongolia, a project called Snow Leopard Enterprises (SLE) helps herder communities earn extra money in exchange for their promise to protect the endangered cat. Women in Mongolian herder communities make a variety of

> Snow leopards are most active at dawn or dusk, but are rarely seen in the wild.

products—yarn for making clothes, decorative floor rugs, and toys—using the wool from their herds. SLE buys these items from herding families and sells them abroad. Herders must agree to protect the snow leopards and to encourage neighbors to do the same.

I The arrangement increases herders' incomes by 10 to 15 percent, and elevates the status of the women. If no one in the community kills the protected animals over the course of a year, the program members are rewarded with a 20 percent **bonus** in addition to the money they've already made. An independent review in 2006 found no snow leopard killings in areas where SLE operates. Today, the organization continues to add more communities.

J Projects like the Homestays program in India and SLE's business in Mongolia are doing well. Though they cover only a small part of the snow leopard's homeland, they make the leopards more valuable to more people each year. If these programs continue to do well, the snow leopard may just have a fighting chance.

A. Choose the best answer for each question.

MAIN IDEA

1. What is the main idea of paragraph C?

    a. Local herders are uncooperative in attempts to save snow leopards.
    b. The snow leopard's endangerment is due in part to the black market.
    c. Snow leopards are killed for their fur and body parts.
    d. It is difficult to enforce the laws made to protect the snow leopard.

REFERENCE

2. In the last sentence of paragraph D, *this trend* refers to _____.

    a. the fall in the snow leopard population
    b. the pressures caused by the black market
    c. increasing conflict with the herders
    d. the opinion of conservationists

DETAIL

3. According to conservationists, what's the best way to save the snow leopard?

    a. create a nature park where they can be free
    b. move herders away from where the snow leopard lives
    c. pass laws to punish people who kill snow leopards for their fur
    d. make people recognize the value of living snow leopards

DETAIL

4. Which of these is NOT true about the Himalayan Homestays program?

    a. The organization helps herders to build fences.
    b. Herders provide accommodations to guests.
    c. Some herders work as nature guides.
    d. Visitors pay a weekly fee to stay at a herder's house.

DETAIL

5. Why is the Mongolian women's status in the community "elevated" (paragraph I)?

    a. They can encourage their neighbors.
    b. They are saving money for the snow leopards.
    c. They are earning money for the community.
    d. They are living higher up in the mountain.

WORDS FROM CONTEXT

B. Find the words in bold in the reading passage. Then choose the correct meaning of each word or phrase.

1. stalks (paragraph A)	a. hunts	b. eats
2. fortune (paragraph C)	a. a little money	b. a lot of money
3. depend on (paragraph E)	a. want	b. need
4. address (paragraph F)	a. solve	b. change
5. incentives (paragraph G)	a. penalties	b. rewards

Annotating a Reading Passage

When you read a passage it can be useful to mark—or annotate—the text. This allows you to focus on the most important information, and makes it easier to see key details when you refer back to the text. Here are some ways to annotate a text:

- Underline new vocabulary and write definitions above the words or in the margin.
- Draw a circle around important names, numbers, statistics, or dates.
- When you find interesting details, note a reaction or a question in the margin.
- Add a question mark next to things you don't understand so you remember to check them later.

Look at the annotations a student made to paragraph B of the reading passage.

> recognizable — Best known for its spotted coat and long <u>distinctive</u> tail, the
> Why? — snow leopard is one of the world's <u>most secretive animals</u>. These
> distant — elusive cats can only be found high in the <u>remote</u>, mountainous
> regions of (Central Asia). For this reason, and because they hunt
> primarily at night, they are very rarely seen.

ANNOTATING **A.** Look back at the reading passage. Add annotations to the section "The Value of Preservation."

B. Work with a partner. Compare your annotations and add any new ones that you think are useful.

CRITICAL THINKING Evaluating

▶ What do you think is the main purpose of the financial incentives offered by the Homestays and SLE programs? Note down your ideas.

_____

▶ How are the incentives of the two programs different? Note down your ideas.

_____

▶ Which of the programs do you think might be more effective? Why? Discuss your ideas with a partner.

A snow leopard at ⟩
the Denver Zoo

DEFINITIONS **A.** Read the information below and match the correct form of each word in **red** with its definition. One word is extra.

The cheetah, known for its **distinctive** spots, sits silently and scans the **landscape** for its prey. Finding a target, it slowly stalks the animal until it is close enough to get its reward. Once the prey is killed, the cheetah **drags** the animal to a safe place.

The cheetah is a natural-born hunter, but, sadly, declining cheetah numbers mean that the animal's **status** is now **officially** listed as vulnerable. To **reverse** the trend, game wardens are working to **enforce** the anti-poaching laws that should protect cheetah populations. It will be a sad day if this beautiful animal disappears from our planet.

^ **Hasari, a three-year-old cheetah, at a U.S. conservation center**

1. in a formal or public way   _____

2. to pull a heavy weight across the ground   _____

3. to change direction, or become the opposite   _____

4. to make sure people obey rules   _____

5. the view around you in the countryside   _____

6. the state of something at a particular time   _____

DEFINITIONS **B.** Complete each sentence. Circle the correct option.

1. If you are in **poverty** you can't support yourself *emotionally / physically / financially*.

2. A **conflict** is a type of *discussion / disagreement / decision*.

3. Someone who receives a **bonus** at work gets *extra money / a promotion / time off*.

4. Something that looks *the same as / similar to / different from* others is **distinctive**.

WORD FORMS **C.** Some words, like **conflict** and **reverse**, can act as nouns and verbs. Complete the sentences with a word from the box. One word is extra.

capture	conflict	contact	reverse	signal

1. _____ between environmentalists and police has delayed the construction of several oil pipeline projects.

2. Recent data provide a clear _____ that Arctic ice is melting rapidly.

3. Some remote tribes in the Amazon have had no _____ with the outside world.

4. Researchers _____ koalas to monitor their heath.

A carer holds a panda cub at a research and breeding center in Sichuan, China.

PROTECTING PANDAS

BEFORE YOU WATCH

DEFINITIONS **A.** Read the information. The words and phrases in **bold** appear in the video. Match each one with a definition.

Most people know that giant pandas **rely on** bamboo as their main food source. However, over two million years ago, giant pandas—like other bears—were actually meat-eaters. It is unclear why giant pandas evolved to live on a **diet** of bamboo. Though panda's jaws are well suited to chewing on bamboo, their stomachs find bamboo hard to **digest**. In addition, while it is high in fiber, bamboo contains very little **protein**. This may explain why pandas conserve their energy for much of the day.

1. **digest** • • food that one regularly eats
2. **protein** • • to process food in the stomach
3. **diet** • • a substance found in some food (such as meat or fish)
4. **rely on** • • to trust in or depend on

PREDICTING **B.** Look at the statements below about giant pandas. Circle if you think the statement is true (T) or false (F). Discuss your ideas with a partner.

1. Giant pandas can spend half of each day eating.   T   F
2. Their black-and-white fur protects pandas from predators.   T   F
3. Giant pandas are an endangered species.   T   F
4. The number of giant pandas has decreased in the last decade.   T   F

VIEWING **A.** Watch the video. Check your predictions in **Before You Watch B**

MULTIPLE CHOICE **B.** Watch the video again. Choose the best option for each question or statement.

1. According to the video, what kind of plant is bamboo?

a. a type of grass   b. a type of tree   c. a type of vegetable

2. Which of the following statements is true?

a. Pandas grow slowly in their first year.

b. Pandas lose most of their dark fur in winter.

c. Pandas today live mostly in mountain areas.

3. According to the video, what is the greatest current threat to wild giant pandas?

a. New predators are entering their habitats.

b. It is becoming more difficult to find enough bamboo.

c. Poachers are killing them for their fur.

CRITICAL THINKING Synthesizing   How are giant pandas and the koalas described in Reading 3A similar? How are they different? Note ideas on the topics below. Then discuss with a partner.

Diet   Habitat   Human threats

Behavior   Environmental threats   Ways they are being helped

VOCABULARY REVIEW

Do you remember the meanings of these words? Check (✓) the ones you know. Look back at the unit and review any words you're not sure of.

Reading A

☐ capture   ☐ extinct   ☐ grasp   ☐ physical*   ☐ primary

☐ reproduce   ☐ signal   ☐ suburb   ☐ tend to   ☐ threaten

Reading B

☐ bonus   ☐ conflict*   ☐ distinctive* ☐ drag   ☐ enforce*

☐ landscape   ☐ officially   ☐ poverty   ☐ reverse*   ☐ status*

* Academic Word List

VIOLENT EARTH

Lava flows down the slopes of
Mount Mayon, the most active
volcano in the Philippines.

4A

DEFINITIONS **A.** Read the caption on this page, and match the words in **bold** with their definitions.

1. (for a volcano) threw out melted rock and smoke _____

2. used to describe a volcano that could erupt at any time _____

3. believed to be related to a god or gods, and given respect _____

4. the powder that is left after something burns _____

PREDICTING **B.** You are going to read about two volcanoes. Look quickly at the title, headings, and captions on pages 58–60. Check (✓) the topics you think you'll read about.

☐ religious beliefs ☐ threats to tourism

☐ why scientists are concerned ☐ recent eruptions

☐ how volcanoes erupt ☐ threats to locals

Mount Fuji, an **active** volcano in Japan, last **erupted** in 1707, sending large clouds of **ash** into the air. Japan's native religion, Shintoism, considers Fuji to be a **sacred** place.

SACRED SUMMITS

A Volcanoes are creators and destroyers. They can shape lands and cultures, but can also cause great **destruction** and loss of life. Two of the best-known examples are found at opposite ends of the world, on the Pacific Ring of Fire.

Symbol of Japan

B It's almost sunrise near the **summit** of Japan's Mount Fuji. Exhausted climbers, many of whom have hiked the 3,776 meters through the night to reach this point, stop to watch as the sun begins spreading its golden rays across the mountain. For the climbers, this is an important moment. They have **witnessed** the **dawn** on Mount Fuji—the highest point in Japan.

C Mount Fuji is a sacred site. Japan's native religion, Shintoism, considers Fuji a holy place. Other people believe the mountain and its waters have the power to make a sick person well. For many, climbing Fuji is also a rite of passage. Some do it as part of a religious journey; for others, it is a test of strength. Whatever their reason, reaching the top in order to stand on Fuji's summit at sunrise is a must for many Japanese. Every July and August, hundreds of thousands attempt to do so.

D Fuji is more than a sacred site and tourist destination, however. It is also an active volcano around which four million people have settled, and it sits just 112 kilometers from the crowded streets of Tokyo. The last time Fuji erupted, in 1707, it sent out a cloud of ash that covered the capital city and darkened the skies for weeks.

E Today, new information has some volcanologists concerned that Fuji may soon erupt again. According to Motoo Ukawa and his associates at the National Research Institute for Earth Science and **Disaster** Prevention, there has been an increase in activity under Fuji recently. This activity may be caused by low-frequency earthquakes. Understanding what causes these quakes may help scientists predict when Fuji will come back to life. In the meantime, locals living near Fuji hold special festivals each year to offer gifts to the goddess of the volcano—as they have for generations—so that she will not erupt and destroy the land and its people below.

Mexico's Threatening Mountain

F Halfway across the globe from Fuji, Popocatépetl—one of the world's tallest and most dangerous active volcanoes—stands just 70 kilometers southeast of Mexico City. Although the volcano (whose name means "smoking mountain") has erupted many times over the centuries, scientists believe its last great eruption occurred around AD 820. In recent years, Popocatépetl is once again threatening the lives of the people near the mountain; in December 2000, almost 26,000 people were evacuated when El Popo—as Mexicans call the mountain—started to send out ash and smoke. As with all active volcanoes, the question is not *if* it will erupt again (an eruption is **inevitable**); the question is *when* it will happen.

G "Every volcano works in a different way," explains Carlos Valdés González, a scientist who **monitors** El Popo. "What we're trying to learn here are the symptoms signaling that El Popo will erupt." These include earthquakes, or any sign that the mountain's surface is changing or **expanding**. The hope is that scientists will be able to warn people in the surrounding areas so they have enough time to evacuate.[1] A powerful eruption could **displace** over 20 million people—people whose lives can be saved if the warning is delivered early enough.

H For many people living near El Popo—especially farmers—abandoning their land is unthinkable. As anyone who farms near a volcano knows, the world's richest soils are volcanic. They produce bananas and coffee in Central America, fine wines in California, and enormous amounts of rice in Indonesia.

I Today, many people continue to see El Popo as their **ancestors** did. According to ancient beliefs, a volcano can be a god, a mountain, and a human all at the same time. To appease[2] El Popo and to ensure rain and a good harvest, locals begin a cycle of ceremonies that starts in March and ends in August. Carrying food and gifts for the volcano, they hike up the mountain. Near the summit, they present their offerings, asking the volcano to protect and provide for one more season.

---

1 If you **evacuate** from a place, you leave as quickly as possible because of danger.
2 If you **appease** people, you try to stop them from being angry by giving them something they want.

"What we're trying to learn are the symptoms signaling that El Popo will erupt."

—Carlos Valdés González

∧ The second-highest peak in Mexico, Mt. Popocatépetl is about 70 km (less than 45 miles) southeast of Mexico City, and can sometimes be seen from the nation's capital.

A. Choose the best answer for each question.

MAIN IDEA

1. What is paragraph C mainly about?

    a. how Mount Fuji became an important religious site

    b. the healing properties of Mount Fuji

    c. reasons people climb Mount Fuji

    d. the visitors to Mount Fuji

DETAIL

2. Which of these statements about Mount Fuji is NOT true?

    a. It is in Japan.

    b. Scientists believe it may erupt soon.

    c. It has erupted recently.

    d. Locals have traditions concerning the mountain.

⌃ **A river of lava flows through a rocky landscape.**

VOCABULARY

3. In paragraph G, line 4, the word *symptoms* could be replaced with _____.

    a. earthquakes   c. sounds

    b. signs   d. lessons

DETAIL

4. What was the reason for the evacuation from El Popo in 2000?

    a. People could see smoke and ash.

    b. People felt the ground shaking.

    c. People saw the surface change shape.

    d. People heard a loud noise.

DETAIL

5. Which statement is true about both Mount Fuji and El Popo?

    a. They have both erupted recently.

    b. They are both less than 100 kilometers from a very large city.

    c. Locals present gifts to both volcanoes for protection.

    d. They both provide rich soil used for producing coffee.

SCANNING FOR INFORMATION

Review this reading skill in Unit 1B

B. Which paragraph of the section "Mexico's Threatening Mountain" contains the following information (1–6)? Write the correct paragraph letter (F–I) next to each piece of information.

1. information about a past eruption _____

2. examples of agricultural products that volcanoes provide _____

3. a definition of a key term or name _____

4. a quote from a volcano expert _____

5. a description of religious practices _____

6. an estimate of how many people could be affected by an eruption _____

Summarizing a Text

After you read a passage, it can be helpful to write a two- or three-sentence summary; this can help you better remember the key points. A good summarizing strategy is to review your annotations (see Unit 3) to see what the main ideas are. Avoid adding unimportant details to your summary.

SUMMARIZING **A.** Read the short passage below. Then write a short summary.

Living Near a Volcano

As world population grows, more people are living in dangerous areas, including near active volcanoes. The Decade Volcano Project has named 16 of these volcanoes as particularly worthy of investigation based on their potential for destruction. The project aims to increase study of these particular volcanoes—their historical timeline for activity, how we can better predict future activity, and, most importantly, what people can do to prepare for an eruption.

▲ **In 1669, lava flows from Mt. Etna reached the city of Catania (foreground).**

It may seem strange to think of "defending" a town against a volcanic eruption, but the project already boasts several successes. For example, during the 1992 eruption of Mount Etna in Sicily, a lava flow was threatening the town of Zafferana. Local authorities blocked the flow in a tube that was feeding lava from higher up the slope. They dropped large blocks of concrete from helicopters into the tube, successfully plugging and diverting the lava.

_____

_____

_____

_____

SUMMARIZING **B.** Write a short summary of the reading passage "Sacred Summits." Compare with a partner and make any improvements to your summary.

CRITICAL THINKING Analyzing Pros and Cons

▶ Why do most local people risk their lives rather than move away from an active volcano? Note down the reasons from the reading.

_____

▶ What do you think local authorities should do? Force people to leave their homes? Build volcano defenses? Something else? Discuss your ideas with a partner.

VOCABULARY PRACTICE

COMPLETION **A. Complete the paragraph with words from the box. One word is extra.**

ancestors	dawn	disastrous	inevitable	summit

Mexicans know lots of ancient stories that have been passed down from their
¹_____—many of these involve volcanoes. "The Legend of Popo" tells the story
of a princess called Iztaccíhuatl and a soldier named Popocatépetl who fall in love. In one
version, Iztaccíhuatl dies of grief after hearing ²_____ news: Popocatépetl has
been killed in battle. But Popocatépetl returns alive; he carries Iztaccíhuatl's body to the
³_____ of a nearby volcano and waits to die. Eventually, snow covers them both
and they become two mountains—Mt. Iztaccíhuatl and Mt. Popocatépetl. Smoke is often
seen at ⁴_____, rising from one of the volcanoes. According to legend, this is
the torch of Popocatépetl.

COMPLETION **B. Complete the paragraph with the correct form of words from the box.**

destructive	displace	expand	monitor	witness

Mt. Kīlauea on Hawaii's Big Island is one of the most
active volcanoes on Earth. Local islanders have been
¹_____ to its evolving shape over hundreds of years.
Sections of earth are often ²_____ by a sudden jolt,
or pressure builds up under the surface as the hot molten
rock ³_____, causing a(n) ⁴_____ eruption.
Nowadays, the volcano is closely ⁵_____ by scientists
trying to predict the next eruption.

⌃ **Tiny rocks from Mt. Kīlauea are known as Pele's tears.**

WORD LINK **C. The word expand contains the prefix ex- which means "away," "from," or "out."
Complete the sentences with the correct word from the box. One word is extra.**

exceed	exit	expand	explosion	export

1. Improved telescopes have _____ our knowledge of the universe.
2. Brazil's biggest _____ are soybeans and coffee.
3. For many, the costs of burning fossil fuels _____ the benefits.
4. A violent _____ almost destroyed the Kīlauea volcano in 2018.

BEFORE YOU READ

TRUE OR FALSE **A.** The map shows the areas that are most at risk of disastrous earthquakes. Read the sentences below and circle **T** (true) or **F** (false).

1. Much of southern Europe has a moderate risk of earthquakes.   **T**   **F**

2. People living along the east coasts of North and South America are often affected by earthquakes.   **T**   **F**

3. Australia has a low or moderate probability of earthquakes.   **T**   **F**

SCANNING **B.** Quickly scan the reading to answer this question: Does the author of this passage think that predicting earthquakes is possible? Then read the passage to check your answer.

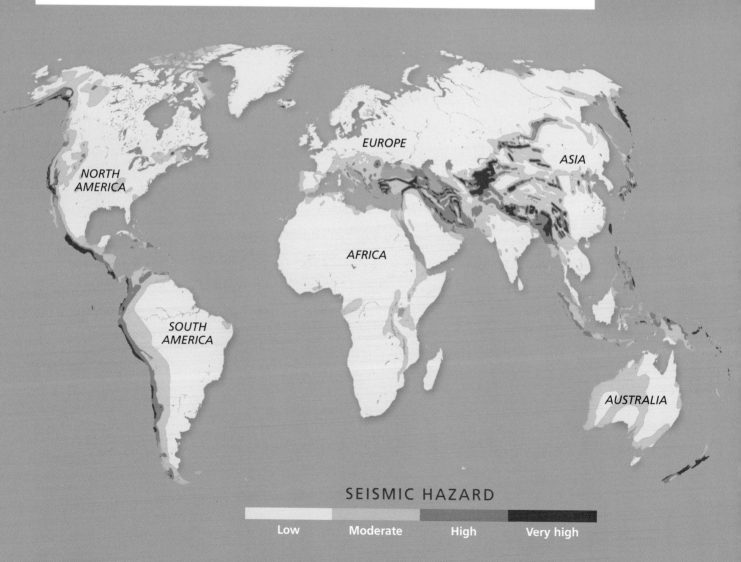

SEISMIC HAZARD

Low   Moderate   High   Very high

IS PREDICTION POSSIBLE?

A   Never before have so many people been packed into cities—places such as Los Angeles, Istanbul, Tokyo, and Lima—that are regularly affected by earthquakes. Located near the edge of Earth's huge, shifting plates, these cities face the risk of serious damage and economic disaster from large quakes—as well as the tsunamis, fires, and other kinds of destruction they often cause.

B   We understand earthquakes better than we did a century ago. Scientists would like to be able to predict them, but is this possible? Today, some of the simplest questions about earthquakes are still difficult to answer: Why do they start? What makes them stop? Perhaps the most important question scientists need to answer is this: Are there clear patterns in earthquakes, or are they basically **random** and impossible to predict?

C   In Japan, government scientists say they have an answer to the question. "We believe that earthquake prediction is possible," says Koshun Yamaoka, a scientist at the Earthquake Research Institute at the University of Tokyo. In fact, Japan has already predicted where its next great earthquake will be: the region of Tokai southwest of Tokyo. Here, two plate boundaries have generated huge earthquakes every 100 to 150 years, but there hasn't been a major quake here since 1854. The theory is that stress is building up in this **zone**, which could lead to a **massive** quake. Unfortunately, this is more a forecast than a prediction. It's one thing to say that an earthquake is likely to happen in a high-risk area. It's another to predict exactly where and when the quake will occur.

D   The desire for a **precise** prediction of time and place has led to another theory: the idea of "preslip." Naoyuki Kato, a scientist at the Earthquake Research Institute, says his **laboratory** experiments show that before a fault in the Earth's crust finally breaks and causes an earthquake, it slips[1] just a little. If we can **detect** these early slips taking place deep in the Earth's crust, we may be able to predict the next big quake.

Clues in the Desert

E   Scientists working in Parkfield, California, are also trying to see if predicting earthquakes is possible. They've chosen the town of Parkfield not only because the San Andreas Fault runs through it, but because it's known for having earthquakes quite regularly—approximately every 22 years. In the late 1980s, scientists in Parkfield decided to study the fault to see if there were any warning signs prior to a quake. To do this, they drilled deep into the fault and set up equipment to register activity. Then they waited for the quake.

---

1 If something **slips**, it slides out of place.

F Year after year, nothing happened. When a quake did finally hit on September 28, 2004, it was years off **schedule**, but most disappointing was the lack of warning signs. Scientists reviewed the **data** but could find no evidence of anything unusual preceding the quake. It led many to believe that perhaps earthquakes really are random events. Instead of giving up, though, scientists in Parkfield dug deeper into the ground. By late summer 2005, they had reached the fault's final depth of three kilometers, where they continued collecting data, hoping to find a clue.

G And then they found something. In an article published in the July 2008 journal *Nature*, the researchers in Parkfield claimed to have detected small changes in the fault shortly before an earthquake hit. What had they noticed? Just before a quake, the cracks in the fault had widened slightly. Scientists registered the first changes 10 hours before an earthquake of 3.0 on the Richter scale[2] hit; they identified identical signs two hours before a 1.0 quake—demonstrating that perhaps the "pre-slip" theory is correct. In other words, it may in fact be possible to predict an earthquake.

H Although there is still a long way to go, it appears from the research being done all over the world that earthquakes are not entirely random. If this is so, in the future we may be able to **track** the Earth's movements and design early-warning systems that allow us to predict when a quake will happen and, in doing so, prevent the loss of life.

---

2 The **Richter scale** is a scale used for measuring how severe an earthquake is.

BUILDING FOR PROTECTION

In many of the world's at-risk cities, new structures are designed to survive earthquakes. However, for older structures, engineers need to innovate. These changes help to make the structures stronger, which will reduce damage and allow for quicker repairs.

1 BOLTED FOUNDATIONS
Wood-framed homes can be attached to foundations using long steel bolts. This makes them less likely to collapse.

2 FLEXIBLE JOINTS
Adding flexible joints can allow tunnels to bend.

3 SHOCK ABSORBERS
Larger buildings can be separated from their foundations and placed on steel and rubber pads. This helps the building better absorb strong shock waves.

4 UTILITY PROTECTORS
Tubes added around water pipes and electrical cables can move when the ground moves. This prevents damage to key utilities and makes repairs easier.

5 MICROPILES AND MESH
Micropiles—long pipes—inserted through the foundations, as well as steel mesh wrapped around the columns, can make bridges and overpasses more flexible.

6 STEEL "SKELETONS"
Steel "skeletons" attached to inner walls allow skyscrapers to sway without breaking.

---

1 If a structure **collapses**, it falls down, usually suddenly and unexpectedly.
2 A **pad** is a cushioned surface.
3 A **mesh** is a thin covering usually made of crisscrossed steel or plastic wires.
4 If something **sways**, it moves from side to side.

LIVING
WITH THE THREAT

WAVES OF DESTRUCTION

An earthquake's waves come in two forms. P-waves (yellow) arrive fastest and compress and punch the rock. S-waves (red) are slower but more destructive. They move from side to side to shake and destroy buildings. At the ground level, P- and S-waves combine to produce surface waves that crack windows and even destroy bridges.

A. Choose the best answer for each question.

GIST

1. What is the reading mainly about?

a. new earthquake-prediction technology
b. earthquake-prediction failures
c. efforts to predict when an earthquake will happen
d. Japan's work on predicting earthquakes

PARAPHRASE

2. Which of the following is closest in meaning to the reading's first sentence, beginning *Never before have* . . . ?

a. Most people in big cities have experienced earthquakes.
b. Cities crowded with people are more likely to have serious earthquakes.
c. Some of the biggest cities in the world suffer damage from earthquakes.
d. More people than ever live in cities that are affected by earthquakes.

∧ **San Andreas Fault, California**

REFERENCE

3. In paragraph E, line 5, what does *do this* refer to?

a. wait for an earthquake
b. study the fault
c. find a fault
d. set up equipment

DETAIL

4. Which of the following statements is NOT true?

a. A major earthquake occurs in Tokai every 100 to 150 years.
b. Scientists believe that the "pre-slip" theory could help predict earthquakes.
c. Data supporting the "pre-slip" theory was found in Parkfield.
d. Scientists recorded a major earthquake in Parkfield in late summer 2005.

MAIN IDEA

5. What is the main idea of paragraph H?

a. Further research will likely help us avoid loss of life in the future.
b. Earthquake research has had a long and successful history.
c. Several kinds of warning systems have been designed to predict earthquakes.
d. It is unlikely we will be able to predict the Earth's movement accurately.

SUMMARIZING

Review this reading skill in Unit 4A

B. Complete this brief summary of the passage with the statements (a-e) that express the most important ideas. Two statements are extra.

Researchers around the world are working out how we can better predict earthquakes.
1 _____   2 _____   3 _____

a. Scientists think underground slips might be warnings of an earthquake.

b. One area near Tokyo has large earthquakes every 100 to 150 years.

c. In California, slight underground movements were identified just before an earthquake.

d. Earthquake strength is usually measured using the Richter scale.

e. Scientists now believe earthquakes are not random and might be predicted.

Analyzing Infographics (2)

Some infographics include descriptive text with photos or illustrations. The purpose of this type of infographic can be to show a chronology of events, compare and contrast information, illustrate steps in a process, or show cause-and-effect relationships. Look for how colors and numbers help connect the visuals to the text.

ANALYZING **A.** Look back at the infographic "Living with the Threat." What information does it show? Circle the two best descriptions (1–5).

1. how new ideas can help protect old structures from earthquakes
2. how earthquakes might one day be predicted in an urban environment
3. how different waves from an earthquake can impact structures
4. why some earthquakes are much more destructive than others
5. why modern structures are safer than older structures

ANALYZING **B.** What innovations are best suited to each of the structures below? Match the innovation (1–6) to the structure (a–f).

1. Steel bolts •   • a. Underground cables
2. Flexible joints •   • b. Very tall buildings
3. Shock absorbers •   • c. Mid-sized buildings
4. Protective tubes •   • d. Small homes
5. Micropiles •   • e. Bridges
6. Steel skeletons •   • f. Subway tunnels

UNDERSTANDING INFOGRAPHICS **C.** Read the caption "Waves of Destruction." Add the labels below next to the correct arrows on the infographic.

P-wave   S-wave   Surface wave

CRITICAL THINKING Evaluating Visual Information   Look again at the infographic. Where do you think is the safest place to be during an earthquake? Mark an X in the safest spot. Note two or three reasons for your choice, and share your ideas with a partner.

_____

_____

_____

VOCABULARY PRACTICE

COMPLETION **A.** Complete the sentences with words from the box.

> **massive**   **random**   **schedule**   **track**   **zone**

1. Earthquakes are hard to predict because they don't seem to follow any regular pattern or _____; they occur almost at _____.

2. Scientists who _____ the movements of the Earth's crust believe that a _____ earthquake, known as "the Big One," will eventually hit southern California.

3. Research after the 2004 Asian tsunami found only two dead buffaloes in a large wildlife conservation _____ in Sri Lanka. This led to renewed belief that animals are sensitive to the near arrival of earthquakes.

COMPLETION **B.** Complete the information with words from the box. One word is extra.

> **data**   **detect**   **foundation**   **laboratory**   **precise**

Researchers conducting experiments in a [1]_____, as well as those observing animals in the real world, suggest that animals are much more aware of the world around them than human beings. For example, some scientists believe that dogs can be used to predict earthquakes. Mitsuaki Ota of Azabu University in Japan claims that dogs can [2]_____ early signs of earthquakes about three hours before they happen. Some scientists are confident that with additional research [3]_____, more [4]_____ predictions are possible.

⌃ **Can some animals sense earthquakes before they happen?**

WORD PARTNERS **C.** The words in the box are frequently used with the noun **schedule**. Complete the sentences with the correct words. Two words are extra.

> **behind**   **busy**   **on**   **regular**   **work**

1. Construction companies prefer building projects to be _____ schedule and under budget.

2. Many office workers complain that they have very _____ schedules with too many meetings.

3. Winter weather can cause trains and buses to run _____ schedule.

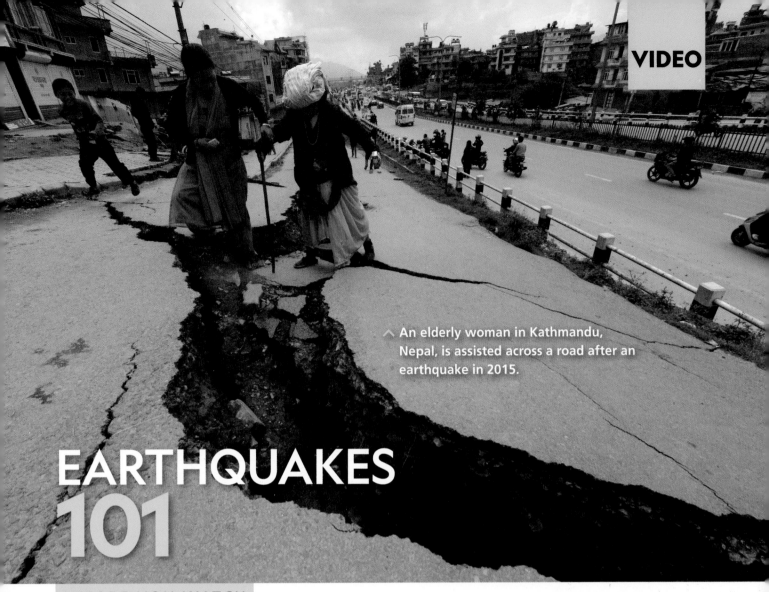

An elderly woman in Kathmandu, Nepal, is assisted across a road after an earthquake in 2015.

EARTHQUAKES
101

BEFORE YOU WATCH

DEFINITIONS **A.** Read the information. The words and phrases in **bold** appear in the video. Fill in the blanks to complete the definitions.

On May 22, 1960, the largest **magnitude** earthquake in recorded history—9.5 on the Richter scale—hit southern Chile. This **devastating** quake left two million people homeless, injured at least 3,000, and killed approximately 1,655. Occurring at a relatively **shallow** depth of 30 kilometers, shockwaves **rattled** houses in cities thousands of miles from the epicenter.

1. Something that is not very deep can be described as _____.
2. When an earthquake is of a large _____, it's very big.
3. If something is _____, its destruction is extreme.
4. When something is _____, it is shaken considerably.

PREDICTING **B.** Do you know how earthquakes begin? Use the words below to discuss your ideas with a partner. Use a dictionary to help you. Check your ideas as you watch the video.

Earth's crust	tectonic plates	movement	shockwaves

GIST **A.** Watch the video. Check (✓) the topics that are covered.

☐ how earthquakes happen

☐ when the next earthquakes will hit

☐ how earthquakes are measured

☐ examples of strong earthquakes

DETAIL **B.** Watch the video again. Choose the best answer for each question or statement.

1. According to the video, what is true about a subduction zone?

a. It's where two tectonic plates are pushed upwards.

b. It's where the most violent earthquakes occur.

2. Which of these earthquakes was more deadly?

a. Nepal, 2015   b. Haiti, 2010

3. According to the video, how many earthquakes each year actually cause damage?

a. 100   b. 10,000   c. 100,000

CRITICAL THINKING Justifying an Opinion   If you were a government decision-maker in an earthquake-affected country, which of the following would you prioritize? Where would you place the most resources? Discuss your ideas with a partner.

reinforcing old buildings

educating the public on earthquake safety

other idea: _____

ensuring new buildings are earthquake-proof

researching ways to predict earthquakes

VOCABULARY REVIEW

Do you remember the meanings of these words? Check (✓) the ones you know. Look back at the unit and review any words you're not sure of.

Reading A

☐ ancestor   ☐ dawn   ☐ destruction   ☐ disaster   ☐ displace*

☐ expand*   ☐ inevitable*   ☐ monitor*   ☐ summit   ☐ witness

Reading B

☐ data*   ☐ detect*   ☐ foundation*   ☐ laboratory   ☐ massive

☐ precise*   ☐ random*   ☐ schedule*   ☐ track   ☐ zone

* Academic Word List

5

ISLANDS AND BEACHES

A natural rock arch frames a view of a beach near Portimão, Portugal.

Discuss these questions with a partner.

1. Why do you think beaches are such popular places to visit?

2. Can you name any famous islands? What do you know about them?

LAND OF FIRE AND ICE

Never mind its chilly name—as a travel destination, Iceland is hot!

BEFORE YOU READ

DEFINITIONS
A. Read the caption and use the correct form of the words in **bold** to complete the definitions below.

1. A(n) _____ is a place that has many visitors because it is interesting or unusual.

2. A(n) _____ event has lots of interesting things happening in it.

3. Something that is _____ makes you admire it because it is great in size or done with great skill.

SCANNING
B. Scan the next page for numbers to complete the information.

ICELAND FACTS

1. Population: approximately _____ people

2. Area: about _____ square kilometers

3. Daylight hours in summer: about _____ hours

4. Annual visitors to Blue Lagoon: _____

A With the Atlantic Ocean to its south and the Greenland Sea to its north, Iceland is Europe's westernmost country, with the world's most northerly capital city, Reykjavík. Over a thousand years ago, Viking explorers **migrated** from northern Europe to Iceland, where they eventually established the world's first parliament.[1] The country's national language can still be traced to the one spoken by the Vikings. Today, Iceland has a population of about 340,000, spread over more than 100,000 square kilometers. Despite its small size, there are many reasons to visit this remarkable country.

City of Culture

B Most visitors' first port of call is Reykjavík, a small and clean city known for its colorful and stylish **architecture**. The city's downtown area is lined with shops, art galleries, cafés, and bookstores. In 2000, Reykjavík was **awarded** the title of Europe's City of Culture, thanks to its art and museum scenes, and lively nightlife.

C The good news for visitors is that Reykjavík's temperatures are fairly mild. Even in the winter, daytime temperatures are usually above freezing. During winter months, nights are long and the northern lights[2] become visible, lighting up the night sky with a **spectacular** natural display. In summer, the country gets almost 22 hours of daylight. During this time, native Icelanders and visitors alike enjoy partying outdoors until dawn.

Hot Springs

D Iceland is one of the most volcanically active nations in the world, with a number of thermal springs around the island. All are heated **naturally** by underground volcanic activity. In fact, Iceland **converts** energy generated by these springs into electricity, which powers and heats people's homes and businesses. As a result, Iceland burns very little fossil fuel, such as oil and gas. Iceland has some of the cleanest air in the world.

E One of Iceland's most popular hot springs is the Blue Lagoon, a huge lake of bright blue seawater just outside Reykjavík. Surrounded by volcanoes and lava fields, the Blue Lagoon receives more than 1.3 million visitors a year. After a long day's sightseeing or a long night of partying, visitors can relax their muscles and release their **tension** in the lagoon's steaming hot water, which has an average temperature of about 38 degrees Celsius. Some believe the waters are able to **cure** certain illnesses and improve skin quality.

Iceland is famous for its **impressive** natural **attractions**, such as the Blue Lagoon thermal lake, as well as its **lively** capital city, Reykjavík.

---

1 The **parliament** of a country is the group of elected people who make or change laws.

2 The **northern lights** ("aurora borealis") are colored lights often seen in the night sky in places near the Arctic Circle.

Caves and Monsters

F Most of the inner part of Iceland is uninhabited[3] and relatively inaccessible. Nevertheless, there is a range of outdoor activities to enjoy elsewhere in the country. This is particularly true along the coasts: "Iceland is an adventure," said Sol Squire, whose Icelandic company organizes adventure trips. "We have Europe's biggest glaciers, active volcanoes, cave explorations, and skiing."

G One of Iceland's most popular attractions is caving. Exploring Iceland's unusual lava caves, most of which formed more than 10,000 years ago, requires only basic caving knowledge and equipment. Ice caves are more challenging, however, and require special clothes and hiking tools. The best-known ice caves are in Vatnajökull—a layer of ice which, at 8,000 square kilometers, is Iceland's—and Europe's—largest glacier. It also happens to be situated just above an active volcano!

H If exploring caves and glaciers doesn't interest you, head south. Just outside the town of Vík, check out[4] the huge rock formations that were once believed to be **monsters** turned into stone. These are a dramatic part of the scenery on one of Iceland's most magnificent black-sand beaches.

The Golden Circle

I And finally, no trip to Iceland would be complete without a visit to the Golden Circle, a pathway northeast of Reykjavík that connects Gullfoss (a huge "Golden Waterfall"), the hot springs region of Geysir, and Thingvellir National Park. The mid-Atlantic fault that runs through Iceland is **literally** pulling the island apart. Nowhere is this more evident than in the Thingvellir Valley, where the land is actually separating and the stony ground beneath your feet frequently shifts. Hold on while you hike!

∧ **A hiker in Iceland explores an ice cave inside a glacier.**

---

3 If a place is **uninhabited**, no one lives there.

4 If you **check out** something, you look at it or try to find out more about it.

A. Choose the best answer for each question.

PURPOSE

1. Who is this passage mainly written for?

    a. a college researcher studying Viking history

    b. a person planning to invest in Iceland's tourist industry

    c. a scientist researching the formation of glaciers

    d. a tourist thinking of visiting Iceland for the first time

DETAIL

2. What are the hot springs of the Blue Lagoon heated by?

    a. solar energy   c. volcanic activity

    b. electrical power   d. fossil fuels

VOCABULARY

3. In paragraph F, the word *inaccessible* could be replaced with _____.

    a. difficult to reach

    b. strangely beautiful

    c. quietly formed

    d. easily seen

DETAIL

4. What is the Golden Circle?

    a. the most popular area to visit in Reykjavík's city center

    b. a scenic walk around the Blue Lagoon

    c. a pathway that connects a park, a waterfall, and hot springs

    d. a road that goes around the coast of Iceland

DETAIL

5. Where is the mid-Atlantic fault most noticeable?

    a. Reykjavík   c. the Blue Lagoon

    b. Thingvellir Valley   d. Geysir

TRUE OR FALSE

B. Are the following statements true according to the passage, or is the information not mentioned? Circle **T** (true), **F** (false), or **NG** (not given).

1. Iceland's Viking settlers mostly came from Norway.   **T F NG**

2. The Blue Lagoon is a freshwater lake.   **T F NG**

3. It's common to see the northern lights in the winter.   **T F NG**

4. Iceland has gas and oil fields in the center of the country.   **T F NG**

5. You need special equipment to explore an ice cave in Iceland.   **T F NG**

6. Temperatures in Reykjavík are usually below freezing.   **T F NG**

7. Most of the population lives in the inner part of the island.   **T F NG**

8. Tourists visiting Vík need to go by boat.   **T F NG**

Summarizing Details on a Map

Maps and diagrams can help you better understand a text by allowing you to see information in a more visual way. As you read a text, try to make connections between the text and the visual(s). It can be helpful to annotate the visual(s) by adding notes and labels, using information from the text.

ANNOTATING   **A.** Use information from paragraph A of the reading to add the missing labels on the map (1–3).

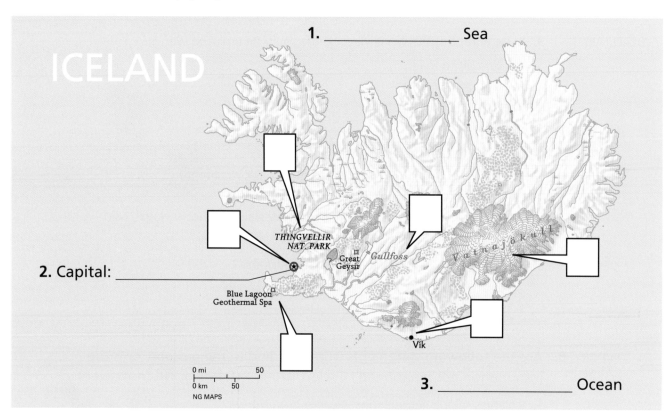

ANNOTATING   **B.** Label each location above with an activity (a–f) that visitors can do there, according to the reading passage.

a. go caving
b. view the mid-Atlantic fault
c. see a large waterfall
d. look at art
e. visit a black-sand beach
f. relax in steaming hot water

CRITICAL THINKING Evaluating Ideas

▶ Which of the activities listed above do you think would be the most interesting? Why? Rank them from 1 (most interesting) to 6 (least interesting).

1. ____   2. ____   3. ____   4. ____   5. ____   6. ____

▶ Compare your rankings with a partner. Imagine you have three days in Iceland together but can only visit four things. Use the map to plan your trip.

COMPLETION **A.** Complete the sentences with the correct form of words in the box.
Two words are extra.

| architectural | award | convert | cure |
| migrate | literally | spectacular | tension |

1. Taroko Gorge on the island of Taiwan is a(n) _____ natural attraction.
2. The Taj Mahal is one of the world's great _____ achievements.
3. The beaches of Bali are a great destination for relieving your _____.
4. Valletta, Malta, was _____ the title of European Capital of Culture in 2018.
5. The mosque in Córdoba, Spain, was _____ to a church in the 13th century.
6. Most researchers believe that Machu Picchu _____ means "Old Mountain."

DEFINITIONS **B.** Read the information. Then complete the definitions using the correct form
of the words in **red**.

1. Most caves are formed **naturally** by the long, slow weathering of rocks.
2. Some scientists believe that some plants in the rain forests of Madagascar contain
   cures for diseases like cancer.
3. A strange creature with flippers and a beak-like mouth, now referred to as the
   "Montauk **monster**," washed up on a New York beach in 2008.
4. The island nation of Singapore was built by people who **migrated** there from
   other countries.

   a. things that restore health _____
   b. a beast-like animal _____
   c. without artificial aid _____
   d. to move to a new or different country _____

WORD WEB **C.** Complete the word web with three words from the box that are synonyms of
spectacular. Use a dictionary or thesaurus, and add other words or phrases with
similar meaning.

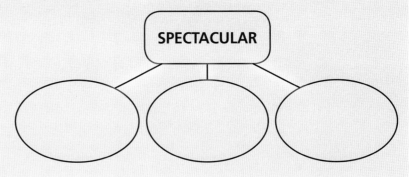

breathtaking
impressive
monotonous
puzzling
satisfactory
stunning

SPECTACULAR

5B

QUIZ **A.** Do you know where these beaches are? Match each beach to its location. Then check your answers on page 88.

1. _____ Copacabana Beach
2. _____ Waikiki Beach
3. _____ Bondi Beach
4. _____ Maya Bay, Phi Phi Island
5. _____ Boracay Beach
6. _____ Miami Beach

a. the Philippines
b. Australia
c. Brazil
d. Thailand
e. Florida, USA
f. Hawaii, USA

SKIMMING **B.** Look at the reading passage's introduction and photo captions. Then answer these questions with a partner.

1. Who is Stanley Stewart, and what is he doing in Brazil?

2. What is your idea of "the perfect beach"? Read the passage to see if Stewart visits a place like the one you've described.

∧ Prainha, one of Brazil's most beautiful beaches

THE PERFECT BEACH

In pursuit of the perfect beach, travel writer Stanley Stewart heads to Brazil, where he discovers some of the world's most beautiful sandy escapes.

A I'm standing on Rio de Janeiro's Copacabana beach, one of Brazil's—and the world's—most famous stretches[1] of sand. As I watch life go by here in all its varied forms, I've come to realize that any understanding of Brazil really begins on its beaches. In this vibrant,[2] multicultural country, the beach is not just a place; it's a **state** of mind—a way of thinking and living.

B Rio alone, I'm told, has over 70 beaches, each with its own community: Some are for bodybuilders, others are for senior citizens, still others are popular with parents and children. But Rio's beaches are just the starting point for my exploration of Brazil's Atlantic coastline, which—at more than 8,000 kilometers, and with more than 2,000 beaches—is the longest in the world. Every Brazilian has his or her own ideas of the perfect beach and is **eager** to tell you where to find it. I'm happy to take people's advice, but my **ultimate** goal is to find my own dream beach.

C I head to a place said to have some of Brazil's best coastline: the state of Bahia in the northeast. Portuguese settlers established themselves at Bahia's present-day capital, Salvador da Bahia, in 1549. Over the centuries, people of many races have arrived and intermarried here, creating a distinctive cultural mix. This mix influences Bahia's language, religion, cuisine, music, and dance.

D I'd been told that one of Bahia's best beaches—Prainha—lies just south of Salvador, near the town of Itacaré. On arriving at Prainha's beach, I discover its golden sand lined by a row of perfect palm trees, moving softly in the ocean breeze. Under the moon, silver waves roll onto the sand. As I enter the water, I have the feeling of swimming through moonlight. Prainha's beauty is **magnificent**—its perfect curves and graceful lines are like something you might see in a postcard. But for me, it's a little too perfect. The beach I'm searching for needs to be a little wilder . . .

---

1 A **stretch** of road, water, or land is a length of it.
2 Something that is **vibrant** is full of life and energy.

E   I continue my search, heading north to one of Brazil's legendary beaches: Jericoacoara. Twenty years ago, only a handful of people were living in Jeri (as it's nicknamed). Today it's an international **destination**, considered one of the best beach hangouts[3] in the world (especially if you like windsurfing). It attracts visitors from Tokyo to Toronto and has grown from a small village into a lively little town. Despite the changes, Jeri hasn't been **spoiled** by tourists, mostly because of its **isolated** location—it's at least five hours from any airport.

F   Everyone in Jeri rents a beach buggy,[4] which comes with a driver. I tell my driver to take me as far along the coast as he can. We drive for three hours, finally arriving at Maceió, a fisherman's beach. Boats lie on their sides while nets hang out to dry on lines between fishermen's houses. We eat on the beach and later rest in hammocks[5] near the table. It's a great day on an amazing beach. *How can it possibly get any better?* I wonder. But I have one final place to visit.

---

3 A **hangout** is a place where a particular group of people gather and relax.
4 A **beach buggy** is a small, open car with large wheels made for driving on a beach.
5 A **hammock** is a piece of strong cloth or netting that is tied between two trees and used as a bed.

G Of the many beach destinations in this country, there is one that all Brazilians hold in high regard—the islands of Fernando de Noronha. More than a dozen beautiful beaches ring the island of Fernando alone, three of which **rank** among the top ten in Brazil. The islands of Fernando de Noronha lie a few hundred kilometers out in the Atlantic. For years, people were **prohibited** from visiting these islands because they were used as a prison and later by the army. Today the islands are a national park and UNESCO World Heritage Site, rich with bird and sea life.

H I visit a number of beaches on Fernando, but I leave the best one for last. The beach at Praia do Leão is the perfect **balance** of sand, sea, and sky. The water is pale blue and warm, alive with colorful fish, turtles, and other marine[6] life; the sand is the color of honey. And in the rock formations and strong winds that occasionally come in from the Atlantic, there is that hint of wildness I was seeking. Finally, I've found the beach of my dreams. I dig my toes in the sand deeply and imagine I can hold on to this place forever.

---

6 **Marine** is used to describe things related to the sea.

Frigatebirds fly over a beach landscape in Fernando de Noronha, Brazil.

A. Choose the best answer for each question.

GIST **1.** What is the reading mainly about?

    a. memories of a childhood vacation

    b. an educational tour of South America's beaches

    c. the author's search for his dream beach

    d. little-known beaches of South America

PURPOSE **2.** What is the purpose of paragraph C?

    a. to describe Bahia's many beaches

    b. to explain why Bahia has the perfect beach

    c. to describe Bahia's music and dance scene

    d. to give information on Bahia's cultural background

INFERENCE **3.** Which of these places is the most isolated?

    a. Copacabana   c. Itacaré

    b. Prainha   d. Praia do Leão

DETAIL **4.** The islands of Fernando de Noronha now _____.

    a. contain a prison   c. are used by the army

    b. are a national park   d. have many beach buggies

REFERENCE **5.** In paragraph H, *the best one* refers to _____.

    a. the collection of Fernando beaches   c. the pale blue water

    b. Praia do Leão   d. the marine life

ANNOTATING MAPS

B. Label the beaches on the map with the best descriptions (1–5) according to the reading passage.

Review This Reading Skill in Unit 5A

1. a good place for fishing

2. a golden beach lined with palm trees

3. a protected national park

4. a world-famous beach by a large city

5. a good place for windsurfing

Identifying a Writer's Point of View

An author's point of view refers to his or her beliefs, opinions, and personal judgments toward a certain subject. In other words, it's how the author feels about what he or she is writing about. An author may have one strong and clear position, or may have conflicting views on the same issue. An author may clearly state how he or she feels, or leave it open to the reader's interpretation. Look for how the author supports his or her point of view—with examples, explanations, and reasons.

IDENTIFYING POINT OF VIEW
A. Look back at the reading passage. Match each place (1–5) to a summary of how Stanley Stewart feels about it (a–f). One summary is extra.

1. Rio _____
2. Prainha _____
3. Jericoacoara _____
4. Maceió _____
5. Fernando de Noronha _____

a. It's a fun place that has not been ruined by its own popularity.
b. It's a beautiful beach, but it's not wild enough.
c. It has different beaches for different types of people.
d. It's a very pretty beach, but there are far too many people on it.
e. It has more than 12 beautiful beaches, one of which has perfect scenery.
f. It's a relaxing beach where you can see how local people live and work.

IDENTIFYING SUPPORTING DETAILS
B. Look back at the passage. Note any examples, explanations, or reasons that Stewart gives to support each of his points of view.

1. Rio _beaches for bodybuilders, senior citizens, parents and children_
2. Prainha _____
3. Jericoacoara _____
4. Maceió _____
5. Fernando de Noronha _____

CRITICAL THINKING Inferring Opinions   Note down your ideas for each question. Then discuss your answers with a partner.

▶ Why do you think Stewart describes Prainha beach as one you might "see in a postcard"?

▶ Stewart describes Prainha as being "a little too perfect." What do you think he means? Is "too perfect" a positive or negative point of view?

▶ Do you know a place that's "a little too perfect"? Describe it.

VOCABULARY PRACTICE

COMPLETION **A.** Complete the information using the correct words in the box. One word is extra.

destination	eager	isolated	state	ultimate

Writer seeks "wife" for a year on a tropical island.

How many women do you think would answer this ad? A 24-year-old British woman named Lucy Irvine did. The opportunity to survive in a(n) ¹_____ place provided her with the ²_____ challenge. The ad was from an adventurer named Gerald Kingsland. As an adventurer herself, Irvine was ³_____ to live on an empty tropical island. Irvine got the job, and not long afterward she was heading for a(n) ⁴_____ on the other side of the world . . .

COMPLETION **B.** Complete the information using the correct form of words in the box.

balance	magnificent	prohibit	rank	spoil	state

The uninhabited island Lucy and Gerald moved to was Tuin, between Australia and Papua New Guinea. As living there was ¹_____ by law, they first needed Australia's permission. When they arrived, the couple was in a complete ²_____ of wonder. The island looked like paradise: a perfect ³_____ of white beaches and clear blue water. However, their experience was soon ⁴_____.
The difficulty of finding drinking water—which ⁵_____ highest on their list of survival needs—forced the pair to set up camp on a less attractive part of the island. Also, their conflicting opinions led to problems. Despite their ⁶_____ surroundings, the adventure lasted only a year.

COLLOCATIONS **C.** The phrases in the box are frequently used with the noun **state**. Complete the sentences with the correct words.

of emergency	of mind	of repair	of shock

1. On hearing very bad news, some people are in a state _____: they don't know what to say.
2. For some older people, age is just a state _____. They still act and behave as they did when they were younger.
3. After a hurricane, local governments often declare a state _____ in places affected by flooding.
4. Because of inadequate funding, some roads and bridges are in a very poor state _____.

HA LONG BAY

View of Ha Long Bay from
Sim Soi Island, Vietnam

BEFORE YOU WATCH

A. Read the information. The words and phrases in **bold** appear in the video. Match the words to their definitions.

A tourist paradise, Vietnam's Ha Long Bay is known for its jewel-like islands circled by **channels** of **emerald** water. The unusual rock formations—called karst towers—are mostly **uninhabited**—except for wildlife such as the rare golden-headed langur.

1. **emerald** •		• a narrow section of sea between two pieces of land
2. **channel** •		• a rich green color like the jewel
3. **uninhabited** •		• without any people living there

GIST **A.** Watch the video. Check (✓) the questions that are answered in the video.

_____ a. What does "Ha Long" mean?   _____ c. How many people visit the bay?

_____ b. How were the rock towers formed?   _____ d. Why are the rock towers unique?

TRUE OR FALSE **B.** Watch the video again. Circle **T** (true), **F** (false), or **NG** (not given).

1. There are over a thousand islands in Ha Long Bay.   **T   F   NG**

2. Most of the islands in Ha Long Bay are populated.   **T   F   NG**

3. According to legend, a dragon attacked the local people.   **T   F   NG**

4. There are two national parks in the area.   **T   F   NG**

5. Ha Long Bay has some of the longest caves in Vietnam.   **T   F   NG**

CRITICAL THINKING Evaluating Using Criteria In 1994, Ha Long Bay was recognized as a UNESCO World Heritage Site. There are two main categories of Heritage Sites: Natural and Cultural. To be included on UNESCO's Natural Heritage list, a site must have one of the following:

– unique natural phenomena   – exceptional natural beauty

– important wildlife habitats   – outstanding natural landforms

▶ Find out if there are any natural places in your country/region on UNESCO's list.

▶ Discuss in a small group: Are there any other natural places in your country/region that UNESCO should include? Note your ideas and share your reasons with another group.

VOCABULARY REVIEW

Do you remember the meanings of these words? Check (✓) the ones you know. Look back at the unit and review any words you're not sure of.

Reading A

☐ architecture   ☐ award   ☐ convert*   ☐ cure   ☐ literally

☐ migrate*   ☐ monster   ☐ naturally   ☐ spectacular   ☐ tension*

Reading B

☐ balance   ☐ destination   ☐ eager   ☐ isolated*   ☐ magnificent

☐ prohibit*   ☐ rank   ☐ spoil   ☐ state   ☐ ultimate*

* Academic Word List

Answers to **Before You Read A**, page 80: **1.** c; **2.** f; **3.** b; **4.** d; **5.** a; **6.** e

6

GLOBAL ADDICTIONS

WARM UP

Discuss these questions with a partner.

1. What things can people become addicted to?

2. Is it okay to be addicted to certain things? If so, what kinds of things?

Video gamers take part in BlitzCon, an annual gaming convention in the USA.

> Most people associate caffeine with coffee, but it can also be found in many other familiar items.

BEFORE YOU READ

MATCHING **A.** How much caffeine do you think is in each item on this page? Match a letter from the chart (**a–h**) to each item. Then check your answers on page 104.

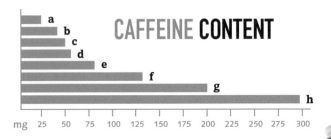

CAFFEINE **CONTENT**

mg 25 50 75 100 125 150 175 200 225 250 275 300

1. Espresso coffee, 30 ml _____b_____
2. Milk chocolate bar, 170 g _____
3. Brewed tea, 240 ml cup _____
4. Can of energy drink, 240 ml _____
5. Brewed coffee, 360 ml cup _____
6. Bottle of cola, 600 ml _____
7. Large soda, 1.9 l _____
8. Pain relief medicine (2 tablets) _____f_____

DISCUSSION **B.** Do you think caffeine is good or bad for you? Read the passage to check your ideas.

7

8

THE WORLD'S FAVORITE DRUG

A It's 1:45 a.m., and 21-year-old Thomas Murphy is burning the midnight oil,[1] studying for an important engineering exam he has at 2:00 in the afternoon later today. To stay awake and alert, he's had two cups of coffee in the last three hours and is now downing a popular energy drink—one that has two to three times the amount of caffeine as a similar sized can of soda. Many students like Murphy, as well as marathon runners, airline pilots, and long-distance travelers, owe their energy to one of humankind's oldest stimulants:[2] caffeine.

▲ **Over two billion cups of coffee are consumed worldwide every day.**

B The power to counter[3] physical fatigue[4] and increase alertness is part of the reason caffeine ranks as the world's most popular mood-altering[5] drug. It is found not only in sodas, energy drinks, coffee, and tea, but in diet pills, pain relievers (like aspirin), and chocolate bars. Many societies around the world have also created entire rituals around the use of caffeine. For example, there's the café culture of France, the tea ceremony in Japan, and the morning cup of coffee or tea that marks the start of the day in many cultures.

C Caffeine is present in many of the foods and drinks we consume, but is it good for us? Charles Czeisler, a scientist and sleep expert at Harvard Medical School, believes that caffeine causes us to lose sleep, which he says is unhealthy. "Without adequate sleep—the typical eight hours—the human body will not function at its best, physically, **mentally**, or emotionally." Too often, Czeisler says, we consume caffeine to stay awake, which later makes it impossible for us to get the rest we need.

D Health risks have also been tied to caffeine consumption. Over the years, studies have attributed higher rates of certain types of cancer and bone disease to caffeine consumption. To date, however, there is no **proof** that caffeine actually causes these diseases.

---

1 If someone is **burning the midnight oil**, they are staying up very late to study or do other work.
2 A **stimulant** is a substance that can temporarily increase the activity of body processes.
3 To **counter** something is to oppose it.
4 **Fatigue** is the feeling of extreme tiredness.
5 A **mood-altering** substance is capable of causing changes in your mood.

E A number of scientists, including Roland Griffiths—a professor at the Johns Hopkins School of Medicine in the United States—believe that regular caffeine use causes physical dependence. Heavy caffeine users, Griffiths says, **exhibit** similar behaviors. For example, their moods fluctuate from high to low, they get mild to severe headaches, or they feel tired or sad when they can't have a caffeinated drink. To minimize or stop these feelings, users must consume caffeine—a behavior Griffiths says is characteristic of drug addiction.

F Despite these concerns, the general opinion in the scientific community is that caffeine is not dangerous when consumed in moderation.[6] This means having one or two small cups of coffee (about 300 milligrams of caffeine) per day, for example. **Furthermore**, a lot of current research **contradicts** long-held negative beliefs about caffeine, and suggests that it may, in fact, have health benefits. For instance, studies have shown that caffeine can help ease muscle pain. Because it is a stimulant, caffeine can also help improve one's mood. Research has also shown that some caffeinated drinks—specifically certain teas—have disease-fighting chemicals that can help the body fight a number of illnesses, including certain types of cancer.

G In addition, as a type of mental stimulant, caffeine increases alertness, memory, and **reaction** speed. Because it fights fatigue, it **facilitates** performance on tasks like driving, flying, and solving simple math problems. And while it is true that caffeine can increase blood pressure, the effect is usually **temporary** and therefore not likely to cause heart trouble. This is especially true if caffeine is consumed in moderation. Moreover, despite its nearly universal use, caffeine has rarely been **abused**. "With caffeine, overuse tends to stop itself," says Jack Bergman, a **specialist** at Harvard Medical School. If you consume too much, "you get . . . uncomfortable, and you don't want to continue."

H Caffeine's behavioral effects are real, but most often mild. Getting that burst of energy, of course, is why many of the world's most popular drinks contain caffeine. Whether it's a student drinking coffee before class or a businessperson enjoying tea with lunch, humankind's favorite stimulant is at work every day, all over the world.

---

6 If you do something **in moderation** (e.g., smoke or drink), you don't do more than is reasonable.

❮ Steamed milk decorates an espresso in what coffee fans call "latte art."

A. Choose the best answer for each question.

GIST **1.** What is this reading mainly about?

    a. recent changes in caffeine consumption

    b. the dangers of caffeine intake

    c. the effects of consuming caffeine

    d. healthy and unhealthy caffeine products

VOCABULARY **2.** In paragraph A, line 7, the word *downing* could be replaced with _____.

    a. holding   c. waking

    b. decreasing   d. drinking

> Coffee trees produce red or purple fruits, sometimes known as "cherries."

INFERENCE **3.** Which statement would sleep expert Charles Czeisler probably agree with?

    a. It's a good idea to consume caffeine if you want to maintain your energy.

    b. Regular consumption of caffeine will make it difficult for you to get enough rest.

    c. How caffeine affects your sleep depends on the type of caffeine you consume.

    d. Caffeine can help you get an adequate amount of sleep if consumed in moderation.

PARAPHRASE **4.** Which of the following is closest in meaning to this sentence from paragraph G?
Moreover, despite its nearly universal use, caffeine has rarely been abused.

    a. Even though caffeine is widely consumed, there aren't many instances of misuse.

    b. Even though caffeine is often misused, it is consumed all over the world.

    c. Because of caffeine's popularity, addiction is a problem.

    d. Caffeine is used all over the world, so it is commonly misused.

COHESION **5.** The following sentence would best be placed at the end of which paragraph?
Many say they couldn't live without it.

    a. Paragraph A   c. Paragraph F

    b. Paragraph D   d. Paragraph G

SCANNING

> Review this reading skill in Unit 1B

B. Match each person mentioned in the reading passage to their conclusions about caffeine.

1. Charles Czeisler _____ _____

2. Ronald Griffiths _____ _____

3. Jack Bergman _____ _____

    a. Caffeine use is not often abused.

    b. Caffeine causes people to lose sleep.

    c. People consume coffee to stay awake.

    d. Caffeine can affect a person's moods.

    e. Regular caffeine consumption can cause dependence.

    f. People often stop consuming caffeine when they have had too much.

Identifying Pros and Cons (1)

A writer may discuss both sides of an argument or an issue. Understanding arguments for an issue (the pros) and the reasons against it (the cons) can help you evaluate the author's claims and determine your position on the issue. The most effective way to do this is to list the pros and cons in two separate columns. This allows you to determine the strength of each claim.

ANALYZING PROS AND CONS

A. Look back at the reading passage. Complete the chart with the pros and cons of caffeine consumption.

Positive Effects	Negative Effects
• counters fatigue and increases alertness • may [1]_____ muscle pain, improves mood • chemicals in some caffeinated drinks can help fight [2]_____ • increases alertness, memory, and [3]_____ speed	• causes us to lose [4]_____ • like being addicted to a [5]_____, causing mood swings, headaches • going without makes us tired and [6]_____ • may increase blood [7]_____ temporarily

EVALUATING PROS AND CONS

B. Answer the questions below with a partner.

1. Read the final paragraph of the reading passage again. Is consuming caffeine a good idea? Why or why not?

2. Look at the chart in activity A. Do you think the reasons for consuming caffeine outweigh the reasons against consuming it? Do you agree with the writer of the reading passage? Explain your answer.

CRITICAL THINKING Evaluating Pros and Cons

▶ Read the statements about eating chocolate candy. Discuss with a partner and note **P** (for pro) or **C** (for con) for each one, or **P/C** if it can be both.

a. _____ It can cause mood swings.

b. _____ It can be expensive if eaten every day.

c. _____ The sugar in chocolate can cause tooth decay.

d. _____ It contains a small amount of caffeine, which can help increase alertness.

e. _____ The calcium in chocolate can reduce the harmful effects of tooth decay.

f. _____ It has a lot of energy-giving calories.

▶ Based on these claims, do you think chocolate is generally positive or negative? What other information or evidence would you want to find out to decide?

COMPLETION **A.** Complete the information below with the correct form of words from the box. One word is extra.

abuse	exhibit	furthermore	proof	reaction

Did you know that you might be ¹_____ your dog if you feed it chocolate? Chocolate can be harmful for dogs and cause a variety of medical problems. A dog's ²_____ to chocolate usually depends on the type of chocolate it is given— dark chocolate is generally worse than milk chocolate. ³_____, a dog is also affected by the amount of chocolate that it consumes. A dog may ⁴_____ symptoms such as rapid breathing, vomiting, or even heart problems if it consumes chocolate.

Source: www.petmd.com

DEFINITIONS **B.** Complete each sentence with the correct answer.

1. If you **facilitate** something, you make it _____.
   a. easier   b. more difficult

2. Something that is **temporary** continues _____.
   a. forever   b. for a limited time

3. A police detective who has **proof** of a crime has _____.
   a. evidence   b. no evidence

4. If something **contradicts** an idea, it _____ it.
   a. opposes   b. supports

5. If you make a **mental** note of something, you _____.
   a. write it down   b. remember it

6. A **specialist** is someone who is _____ in a particular area.
   a. very knowledgeable   b. very well-known

WORD WEB **C.** Complete the word web with words and phrases that are synonyms of **furthermore**. Use a dictionary to help.

BEFORE YOU READ

DISCUSSION **A.** How much time do you spend every day doing the following activities on your phone or other electronic devices? Discuss your answers with a partner.

1. reading articles
2. texting or chatting with friends
3. checking or posting on social media
4. watching videos
5. playing video games

PREDICTING **B.** Look at the photo and read the caption. What are some possible positive and negative effects of using digital technology? Discuss your ideas with a partner. Then read the passage to check your ideas.

ADDICTED TO DISTRACTION

A David Strayer never texts or talks on a phone when he is driving. Strayer is a cognitive psychologist[1] at the University of Utah who specializes in attention. His research shows that, when driving, using a phone can be as dangerous as drinking alcohol.

B Strayer and other scientists warn against multitasking. When we do many things at the same time, Strayer says, our brain becomes tired easily. We make mistakes and lose **focus**. Yet multitasking is increasingly common, especially on a phone or computer. Dr. Gloria Mark, a digital media researcher, has found that people in the United States **switch** tasks on their computers 566 times a day. This type of multitasking is especially common among teenagers. On average, a teenager spends between 7 and 11 hours a day in front of a screen—doing homework, texting, watching videos—often all at the same time.

C Phones, tablets, and laptops are all useful tools, and we may feel more productive when we use them. However, when we spend hours on digital devices—**constantly** switching between activities—our overall productivity decreases. Why?

D Many digital activities require high levels of **concentration**. When we text or email someone, for example, or even play games, we have to focus. When we do this, our brain uses energy. When we multitask—which is hard for the brain to do—we use even more energy. **Excessive** multitasking reduces our ability to think clearly and creatively, and to remember information. This, **in turn**, can result in stress.

E What is the best cure for our overstressed minds? David Strayer says the answer is simple: Spend some time in nature.

Digital technology helps us perform many tasks—often at the same time. But is it affecting our ability to think clearly?

---

1 A **cognitive psychologist** studies the mind and how we learn and remember information.

Directed Attention

We need to concentrate to solve problems and complete tasks. Focusing our attention requires mental energy. When we multitask, we use a lot of energy. This effort can cause mental fatigue and stress.

A Natural Remedy

F Strayer and other scientists are studying nature's effect on our brains and bodies. When we are in natural environments, the prefrontal cortex (the brain's control center) relaxes. Studies show that when people can see trees and grass, they are calmer and do better in school. Indeed, people even relax when they look at *photos* of nature. **Consequently**, they do better on different cognitive tasks.

G Other psychologists are also studying "nature **therapy**." In a study at Chiba University in Japan, 84 subjects went for a 15-minute walk in seven different forests. The same number of people walked around different city centers. Researchers then took blood from each person. The forest walkers had a 16 percent decrease in the stress hormone[2] cortisol. In addition, they had a 2 percent drop in blood pressure and

---

2 A **hormone** is a chemical substance produced in the body that controls the activity of certain cells or organs.

Relaxed Attention
When we spend time in a peaceful, natural environment, we don't have to concentrate on anything specific. This mental break allows the brain to relax, improves short-term memory, and can increase creativity almost 50 percent.

a 4 percent drop in heart rate. All did better than the city walkers. Lead researcher Yoshifumi Miyazaki has an explanation for these results. Our bodies relax in pleasant, natural **surroundings**, he says. Humans evolved in that environment, not in places with tall buildings and lots of traffic.

H Psychologist Stephen Kaplan and his colleagues have done similar research. In one study, people took a 50-minute walk in a public garden. In a test conducted afterwards, their short-term memory improved. When the same people walked on a city street, it did not.

I Kaplan says it is the **visual** details in nature—sunsets, streams, butterflies—that reduce stress and mental fatigue. We enjoy them without having to concentrate on them. This allows our brains to rest and recover from the stresses of modern life. "Imagine a therapy that was readily available, and could improve your cognitive functioning at zero cost," Kaplan says. "It exists: it's called 'interacting with nature.'"

A. Choose the best answer for each question.

MAIN IDEA

1. Which statement best summarizes the main idea of the passage?

  a. Research shows that spending time in nature can reduce stress.
  b. Long working hours are a contributor to rising levels of stress.
  c. More people today are exploring their natural surroundings.
  d. For an improved lifestyle, people should consider moving away from cities.

INFERENCE

2. An example of *multitasking* is _____.

  a. watching a movie with a group of friends
  b. taking a lot of photos during a visit to a park
  c. visiting a number of cities during a road trip
  d. making a phone call while typing an email

PURPOSE

3. What is the writer's main purpose in paragraph D?

  a. to explain why people often play games to reduce stress
  b. to show why certain activities require a lot of focus
  c. to describe how multitasking can affect the brain
  d. to give an example of what *multitasking* means

CAUSE-EFFECT

4. Which of the following is NOT mentioned as a likely benefit of seeing nature?

  a. better school performance   c. faster reaction speeds
  b. improved cognitive ability   d. feelings of calm and relaxation

REFERENCE

5. At the beginning of the third sentence of paragraph I, *This* refers to _____.

  a. enjoying nature   c. concentrating
  b. becoming stressed   d. memorizing

NOTES COMPLETION

B. Complete the research notes using information from paragraph G. Use one or two words or a number from the passage for each answer.

Method

- study conducted by researchers at ¹_____
- groups went for a ²_____-minute walk in different surroundings
- one group walked in various ³_____; another walked in forests
- researchers then tested participants' ⁴_____

Results

- people who walked in ⁵_____ had a ⁶_____ percent drop in cortisol levels (a type of ⁷_____)
- also had a slight decrease in heart rate and ⁸_____

Conclusion

- the human body ⁹_____ in natural environments as we have ¹⁰_____ to be in those surroundings

Understanding Transitions

Transitions are words and phrases used to connect one idea to the next. They help texts flow more smoothly. Transitions have different purposes. Look at the following sentences and the different types of transitions they contain.

She felt very stressed. **However**, *she felt very confident.* (contrast)

She felt very stressed. **As a result**, *she hadn't slept the night before.* (consequence)

She felt very stressed. **In fact**, *she had never felt more stressed.* (emphasis)

CLASSIFYING **A.** Complete the chart with the transitions from the box. Add any other transition words or phrases you know.

above all   in short   likewise   moreover   therefore   yet

To add information	To contrast ideas	To show another similar idea
furthermore in addition	however nonetheless	similarly in the same way

To emphasize a point	To show a consequence	To make a conclusion
in fact indeed	as a result consequently	to conclude ultimately

B. Complete these excerpts using appropriate transition words and phrases from **A**. Then compare your answers with the transitions the writer used in the passage. Do your choices have a similar meaning to the writer's? Discuss with a partner.

1. Studies show that when people can see trees and grass, they are calmer and do better in school. _____, people even relax when they look at *photos* of nature. _____, they do better on different cognitive tasks. (paragraph F)

2. The forest walkers had a 16 percent decrease in the stress hormone cortisol. _____, they had a 2 percent drop in blood pressure and a 4 percent drop in heart rate. (paragraph G)

CRITICAL THINKING Applying Ideas   Note answers to the questions, and discuss with a partner.

▶ If someone lives in the middle of a city, what are the best ways to reduce stress?

_____

▶ What technology (for example, apps) can be used to help reduce stress?

_____

COMPLETION   **A.** Complete the information with the correct form of the words in the box. Two words are extra.

concentration	**consequently**	**constant**
surroundings	**switch**	**therapy**

Perhaps no country has embraced the benefits of interacting with nature more than South Korea. As in many countries, some Koreans suffer from high levels of stress. This can lead to poor

[1]_____, mental fatigue, and even depression. [2]_____, many South Koreans take advantage of nearby "healing forests"—places where they can relax in natural [3]_____. People can benefit from a number of [4]_____—including forest meditation for pregnant women and woodcrafts for cancer patients.

∧ **Anti-stress therapy in a forest near Seoul, South Korea**

DEFINITIONS   **B.** Match the definitions (1–6) to words from the box.

constantly	**excessive**	**focus**	**in turn**	**switch**	**visual**

1. one after the other   _____
2. relating to sight   _____
3. ability to concentrate   _____
4. too much   _____
5. to change suddenly   _____
6. without ending   _____

WORD LINK   **C.** The word root *vis* means "see," as in the word **visual**. Complete the sentences with the correct words in the box. One word is extra.

invisible	**revise**	**vision**	**visual**	**visualize**

1. Eyeglasses help people with poor _____ see better.
2. To improve their writing, authors _____ their work again and again.
3. Fairyflies can be as small as 0.5 mm in length—almost_____ to the naked eye.
4. Some therapists tell patients to _____ their personal goals in their mind.

WORLD OF CAFFEINE

∧ Judges test the quality of coffee during the U.S. Barista Championships.

BEFORE YOU WATCH

DEFINITIONS
A. Read the information. The words and phrases in **bold** below appear in the video. Match the words with their definitions.

Sales of energy drinks—a sweet soda **infused** with caffeine—have increased significantly in recent years. Often containing twice as much caffeine as coffee, energy drinks have especially **caught on** with students, who use the drinks to help stay awake longer to study. As with other caffeinated **beverages**, however, drinking too many energy drinks can result in side effects such as migraines[1] and tremors.[2] In extreme cases, energy drinks may be **lethal**—in 2000, a student in Ireland died after consuming several cans before a basketball game.

1 A **migraine** is a severe headache that lasts a long time.
2 A **tremor** is shaking, usually in the hands, caused by weakness, stress, or illness.

1. infuse •   • a. a prepared drink
2. beverage •   • b. able to cause death
3. catch on •   • c. to become popular
4. lethal •   • d. to add to and soak in a liquid

PREVIEWING
B. How often do you eat or drink these caffeine-based products? Compare your answers with a partner.

| black tea | chocolate | coffee | cola | energy drink |

GIST **A.** Watch the video and complete the statements. Check (✓) all answers that are true.

1. This video is mostly about _____.

- [ ] a. medical explanations of caffeine addiction
- [ ] b. the history of caffeine consumption
- [ ] c. some pros and cons of caffeine consumption

2. According to the video, caffeine is a substance that _____.

- [ ] a. occurs naturally in some plants
- [ ] b. may lead to health problems
- [ ] c. can now be produced in a laboratory

DETAIL **B.** Watch the video again and complete the missing information in the timeline.

3000 BC	1400 BC		15th–16th centuries	mid–18th century
☐	☐		☐	☐

3000 BC   2000 BC   1000 BC   0   1000   1500   2000

a. Coffee became popular in the Ottoman Empire.
b. Cocoa was first consumed by Mesoamericans.
c. Tea was first drunk in China, according to legend.
d. Tea became popular in Britain.

CRITICAL THINKING Evaluating Pros and Cons   In many countries, coffee and tea establishments are open for long hours, and are popular places for social gatherings. What might be some pros and cons of this? For example, consider the following areas:

the economy	personal health	social interaction	academic study

VOCABULARY REVIEW

Reading A

- [ ] abuse
- [ ] contradict*
- [ ] exhibit*
- [ ] facilitate*
- [ ] furthermore*
- [ ] mental*
- [ ] proof
- [ ] reaction*
- [ ] specialist
- [ ] temporary*

Reading B

- [ ] concentration*
- [ ] consequently*
- [ ] constant*
- [ ] excessive
- [ ] focus*
- [ ] in turn
- [ ] surroundings
- [ ] switch
- [ ] therapy
- [ ] visual*

* Academic Word List

Answers to **Before You Read A**, page 90: **1.** b; **2.** a; **3.** c; **4.** e; **5.** g; **6.** d; **7.** h; **8.** f

ENERGY
SOLUTIONS

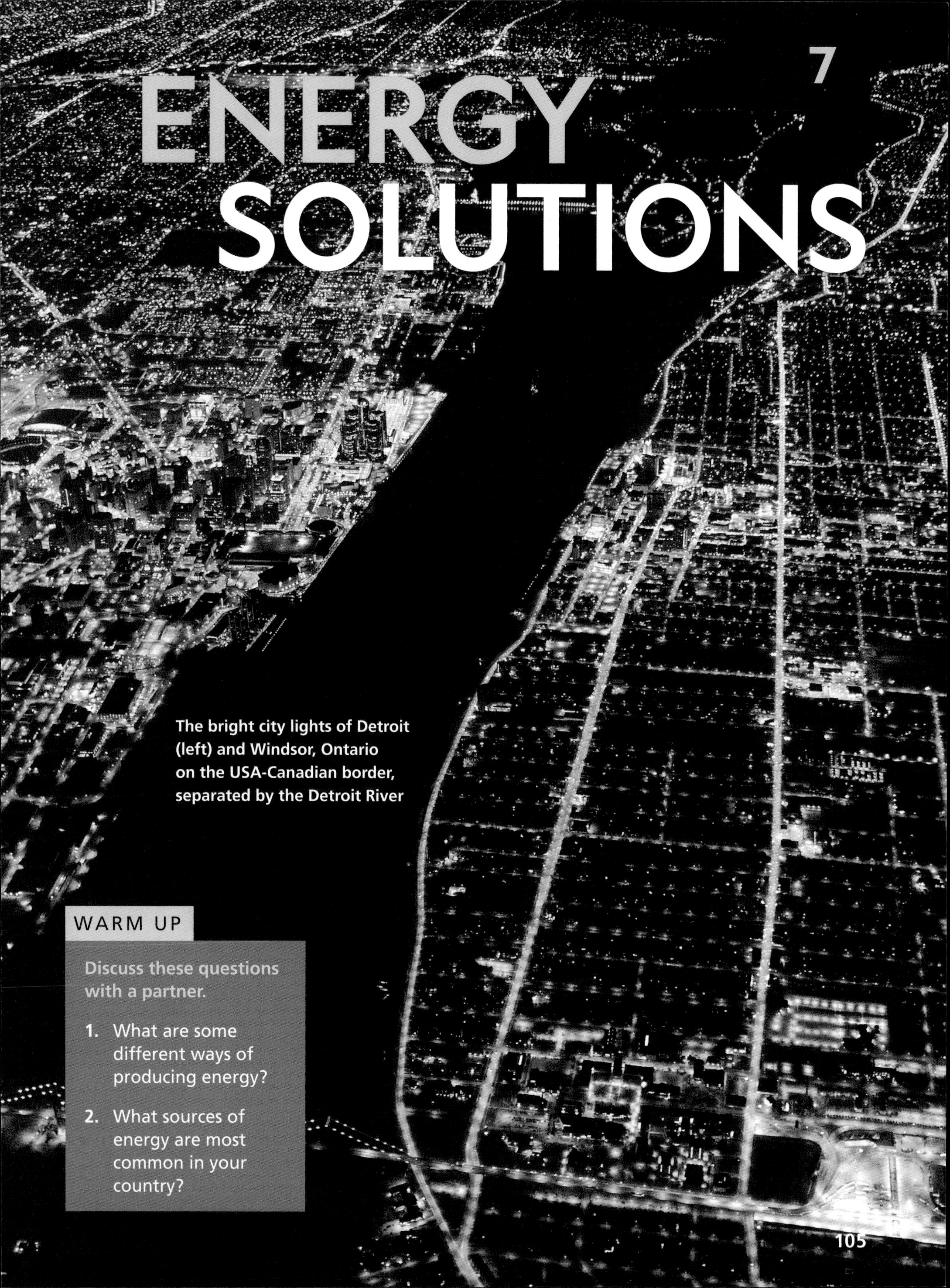

The bright city lights of Detroit
(left) and Windsor, Ontario
on the USA-Canadian border,
separated by the Detroit River

WARM UP

Discuss these questions
with a partner.

1. What are some
   different ways of
   producing energy?

2. What sources of
   energy are most
   common in your
   country?

Aerial view of Solar One, a 10-megawatt solar thermal plant in Daggett, California

BEFORE YOU READ

DISCUSSION **A.** Look at the photo and caption, and answer the questions.

1. What are some advantages and disadvantages of solar power?

2. Aside from solar power, what are some alternative ways of producing energy?

SCANNING **B.** Scan the reading passage. Which countries mentioned in the passage use the alternative energy sources below?

solar   wind   nuclear

_____   _____   _____

POWERING THE PLANET

A Despite modern society's heavy dependence on fossil fuels for energy, most people are aware that the supply of these fuels is finite. As oil and other fossil fuels become more costly and difficult to find, researchers are looking at alternative energy sources, including solar, wind, and even nuclear power. But which **substitute**—if any—is the right one?

Solar

B Solar panels catch energy directly from the sun and convert it into electricity. One of the world's largest solar power stations is in the Indian state of Tamil Nadu, where more than 2.5 million solar panels have the **capacity** to generate enough power for 750,000 people. But unlike the burning of fossil fuels, the process used to create all that solar energy produces no emissions.

C Today, however, solar power provides less than 2 percent of the world's energy, primarily because the cost of the panels is still very high. But price is only one issue. Clouds and darkness also cause solar panels to produce less energy. This requires that additional power sources (such as batteries) be available.

D Some scientists think the solution to this problem can be found in space, which is the ideal place to gather energy from the sun. With no clouds and no nighttime, a space-based solar power station could operate constantly. These stations would send the power back to Earth, which could then be turned into electricity for consumption. Advocates of solar space stations say this technology would initially require a lot of money, but eventually it could provide continuous, clean energy that would be cheaper than other fuels. Also, unlike other energy sources, solar power from space would last as long as the sun shines, and would **guarantee** everyone on Earth all the energy they need.

Wind

E Wind—the fastest-growing alternative energy source—is another way of collecting energy from the sun. Wind is caused by the sun's heat rather than its light. Therefore, unlike solar power, wind power works well even on cloudy days.

F All over the world, incentives designed to decrease the dependence on oil and coal have led to a **steep** increase in wind-powered energy. Today, Asia leads the world in wind power, producing around 230,000 megawatts,[1] the **equivalent** of 230 large coal-powered plants. Europe produces nearly 180,000 megawatts. North America remains a distant third, at 105,000.

G Despite its successes, some people are **protesting** wind-power development, saying the turbines[2] are both noisy and ugly. Just outside England's Lake District—a protected national park—a dozen existing wind towers are due to be removed. "This is a high-quality landscape," says one local homeowner. "They shouldn't be putting those things in here."

H There are other challenges, too. If the wind doesn't blow, the turbines are not able to produce adequate energy. As a result, other power sources are needed. In contrast, a strong wind can create too much power. In cases like this, the energy company must sell the extra power at a much-reduced rate, which is not good for business.

I What's needed for both wind and solar is a way to store a large energy surplus.[3] However, most systems are still decades away from making this a reality. On the plus side, both wind and solar

---

1 A **megawatt** is a unit of power.
2 A **turbine** is a machine that uses water, steam, or wind to turn a wheel to produce electricity.
3 If you have a **surplus** of something, you have more of it than you need.

power enable people to generate their own energy where they live: People can have their own windmills or solar panels, with batteries for calm days.

Nuclear

J In the 1970s, nuclear power was seen as the main energy alternative. Nuclear power produces vast amounts of electricity more cheaply than gas or coal, with no carbon emissions. For a number of years in the 1980s and '90s, however, use of nuclear power **declined** due to accidents, concerns about nuclear waste storage and **disposal**, and high construction costs.

K Today, times are changing. Worldwide, about 450 plants generate 11 percent of the planet's electric power, and some countries have invested heavily in nuclear energy. France, for instance, gets three-quarters of its electricity from nuclear power, the highest percentage of any country. China has started to build one or two new plants a year, and India has also begun to **utilize** nuclear energy on a large scale.

L However, there are still concerns about the safety of nuclear power, as seen, for example, at the Fukushima nuclear power plant in Japan. The country had to close the nuclear reactors at Fukushima when the plant was hit by a tsunami and, as a consequence, began releasing substantial amounts of radioactive materials. Many still believe, however, that nuclear power is one of the future's greenest energy alternatives.

M In the end, are any of these sources alone the answer to our current energy problems? The short answer is no, but used in some combination—along with other power sources— we may find ways to reduce and eventually **eliminate** our dependence on fossil fuels.

Wind turbines on Pillar Mountain, Kodiak, Alaska

A. Choose the best answer for each question.

GIST   **1.** What is this reading mainly about?

     a. possible replacements for fossil fuels
     b. the various causes of the global energy crisis
     c. the benefits of solar power over other alternate energy sources
     d. problems caused by our overdependence on fossil fuels

DETAIL   **2.** Which of these statements about solar energy is stated in the text?

     a. Solar is currently the biggest contributor to the world's energy.
     b. Solar energy is cheap to produce due to the low price of solar panels.
     c. Solar space stations could be the solution to the energy crisis.
     d. Solar energy can have a harmful effect on the environment.

DETAIL   **3.** What is NOT mentioned as a disadvantage of wind power?

     a. Strong winds can produce too much power.
     b. Strong winds can damage the turbines.
     c. The turbines can create a lot of noise.
     d. Some people consider the turbines to be ugly.

DETAIL   **4.** Which country gets most of its power from nuclear power?

     a. France   c. India
     b. Japan   d. China

PARAPHRASE   **5.** Which question is closest in meaning to *In the end, are any of these sources alone the answer to our current energy problems?* (paragraph M)

     a. Is there an energy source that can solve all of our energy problems on its own?
     b. Can our current energy problems be solved by making sure we stop burning fossil fuel?
     c. Can we solve our energy problems by using all the alternative energy sources together?
     d. Is finding an alternate to fossil fuels the only way to solve our energy problems?

MATCHING   **B. Match each energy source with the correct statements(s) (a–f) according to the reading passage. One statement is extra.**

1. Solar   ____ ____   a. Its use declined, but is now gaining popularity.

                        b. Its development has been welcomed by locals.

2. Wind   ____   c. It has the potential to produce energy from space.

                        d. It provides less than 2 percent of the world's electricity.

3. Nuclear ____ ____   e. There have been recent concerns about its safety.

                        f. It is the fastest-growing alternative energy source.

Identifying Pros and Cons (2)

A writer sometimes presents the pros and cons of three or more related ideas. Using a chart to compare the advantages (or disadvantages) of each idea can show you which of them may be the most (or least) beneficial.

IDENTIFYING PROS **A.** Look back at the reading passage. Check (✓) the energy sources used today that have these advantages (1–3).

Advantages	Solar Energy	Wind Energy	Nuclear Energy
1. Has constant power supply			
2. Produces no carbon emissions			
3. Can be produced by people at home			

IDENTIFYING CONS **B.** Look back at the reading passage. Check (✓) the energy sources that have these disadvantages (1–3).

Disadvantages	Solar Energy	Wind Energy	Nuclear Energy
1. Is affected by weather conditions			
2. Has a history of safety issues			
3. Has high construction costs			

CRITICAL THINKING Evaluating Pros and Cons Discuss the following questions with a partner.

▶ Which of the three energy sources do you think has the most significant advantages? Which has the most significant disadvantages?

▶ Which disadvantages do you think will be the easiest to solve? Explain your answer.

▶ Which of the three energy sources do you think is the best option to replace fossil fuels? Why?

> **Nuclear power plant at Three Mile Island, Pennsylvania**

COMPLETION

A. Complete the information using the words from the box. Two words are extra.

Pulau Ubin, Singapore

capacity	eliminate	equivalent
steep	substitute	utilize

In 2010, in an effort to eventually ¹_____ its dependence on fossil fuels, the government of Singapore decided to ²_____ some of its traditional energy production with renewable energies. As part of this initiative, it has turned Pulau Ubin—a small, undeveloped but inhabited island—into a "green island." The island is now powered entirely by clean and renewable energy: It uses the ³_____ amount of electricity as it did before, but without using fossil fuels. It is hoped that other places in the region can fully ⁴_____ green energy so they, too, can become "green islands."

WORDS IN CONTEXT

B. Complete each sentence with the correct answer.

1. If you **protest** an action, you are _____ it.
   a. for
   b. against

2. If a country's energy **capacity** increases, it _____ more energy.
   a. needs
   b. can produce

3. Over the last 100 years, _____ has been **declining**.
   a. environmental quality
   b. the world's population

4. A **steep** rise in prices takes place over a _____ period of time.
   a. short
   b. long

5. If you **guarantee** someone a pay raise, you _____ them more money.
   a. promise
   b. refuse

6. If you **dispose** of something, you _____.
   a. throw it away
   b. store it

WORD PARTNERS

C. The nouns in the box are frequently used with the adjective **steep**, e.g., "a steep climb." Add an arrow for each to show an upward (↑) or a downward (↓) movement.

climb ___	decline ___	dive ___	drop ___	increase ___	reduction ___

BEFORE YOU READ

COMPLETION **A.** Read the photo caption, and complete the sentences using the words or phrases in **bold**.

1. The _____ of a place is its overall environmental impact.

2. If you _____, you do something to achieve a goal.

3. A very large city can be referred to as a(n) _____.

PREDICTING **B.** In what ways do you think a large, modern city like Dubai can reduce its ecological footprint? Discuss your ideas with a partner. Check as you read the passage.

∧ Ski Dubai is the Middle East's first indoor ski park—one of several projects that have turned Dubai into a major **metropolis**. But this growth has an environmental cost, largely due to the city's dependence on fossil fuels. Now Dubai is looking to **take action** to reduce its **ecological footprint**.

CITY OF THE FUTURE?

A To appreciate the audacity[1] of Dubai, you could start by going skiing. The ski resort, located inside one of the city's shopping malls, looks from the outside like a silver spaceship. You put on a thick coat, pull on your gloves—and then marvel at what strong air-conditioning can do. At the exit, you can buy a souvenir T-shirt. A cartoon thermometer in Celsius announces: "I went from +50 to minus 8!"

B Indoor skiing in the desert has become a symbol of Dubai's status as a **wealthy**, modern metropolis. Originally a small fishing village, Dubai's fortunes changed forever with the discovery of oil in the 1960s. Since then, it has evolved to become the largest city in the United Arab Emirates, with over three million residents, huge shopping malls, and a hundred high-rise towers. But the rapid growth has come at a price. To power its cars and air-conditioning, the city has produced large amounts of carbon dioxide (CO_2) from fossil fuels. By 2006, Dubai had one of the largest ecological footprints in the world. But now it is making some big changes.

C To reduce its dependence on cars and lower its **emissions**, Dubai has invested in solar energy, green buildings, and a **comprehensive** public transportation system. Gleaming driverless trains now run beside the main roads. In addition, all new buildings must meet strict energy **regulations**. Smart lighting and **cooling** systems must switch off when no people are present in a room. New buildings must also use solar panels for water heating. "The leadership has recognized that the growth of the economy is not **sustainable** without taking action on emissions," says Tanzeed Alam, a climate and energy specialist.

D The most striking development can be found where the city's suburbs meet the desert. Unlike much of Dubai, the Sustainable City to the south feels more like a close-knit[2] village community. About five hundred low-rise houses are **distributed** along attractive, tree-lined streets. They all face north, away from direct sunlight, and are close together to provide natural shade. Each building has reflective[3] windows and wall paint, which reduce the

---

1 **Audacity** is a willingness to be bold and daring.
2 A group of people that is **close-knit** is tightly connected.
3 If a surface is **reflective**, it casts back light or heat.

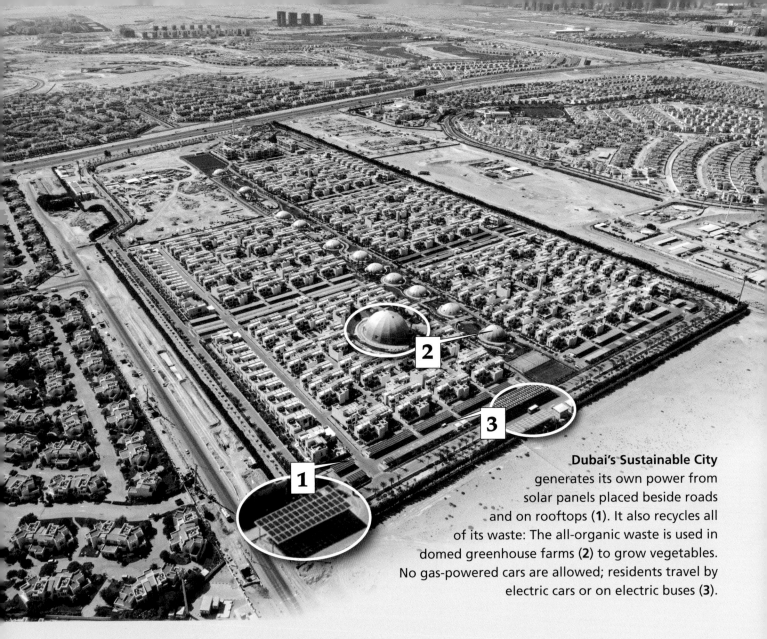

Dubai's Sustainable City generates its own power from solar panels placed beside roads and on rooftops (**1**). It also recycles all of its waste: The all-organic waste is used in domed greenhouse farms (**2**) to grow vegetables. No gas-powered cars are allowed; residents travel by electric cars or on electric buses (**3**).

heat absorbed from the sun. Rooftop solar panels and energy-saving lights contribute to the community's energy **efficiency**. As a result, **residents** of the Sustainable City now consume 50 percent less energy than people living in other parts of Dubai.

E A decade ago, the idea of a fully sustainable community was thought to be **unrealistic**. But times have changed, says Faris Saeed, one of the creators of the Sustainable City. So, too, have prices. The cost of living in the Sustainable City is similar to some of Dubai's other neighborhoods. "It's a myth[4] that sustainable has to be more expensive," Saeed says.

F Dubai's leaders hope the Sustainable City will become a model for the future. By 2050, the government intends to obtain 75 percent of the city's energy from renewable sources—mainly solar. It also wants to have the smallest ecological footprint in the world. The plan is audacious. But if successful, even guilt-free skiing in the desert could become an environmentally sustainable reality.

---

4 A **myth** is a widely held but false belief or idea.

WHAT MAKES A GREEN BUILDING?

Though standards for green buildings vary, they are generally designed to use less energy and water and improve the indoor environment, including air quality.

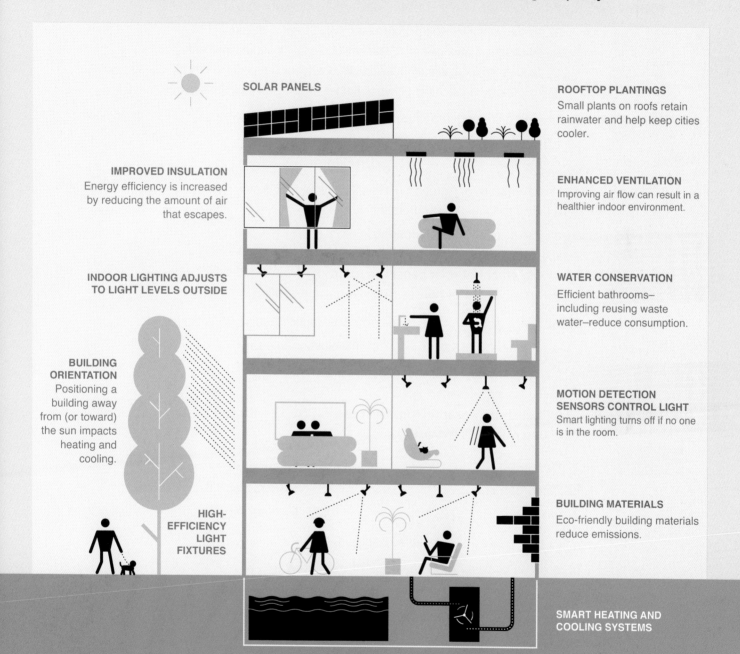

SOLAR PANELS

ROOFTOP PLANTINGS
Small plants on roofs retain rainwater and help keep cities cooler.

IMPROVED INSULATION
Energy efficiency is increased by reducing the amount of air that escapes.

ENHANCED VENTILATION
Improving air flow can result in a healthier indoor environment.

INDOOR LIGHTING ADJUSTS TO LIGHT LEVELS OUTSIDE

WATER CONSERVATION
Efficient bathrooms—including reusing waste water—reduce consumption.

BUILDING ORIENTATION
Positioning a building away from (or toward) the sun impacts heating and cooling.

MOTION DETECTION SENSORS CONTROL LIGHT
Smart lighting turns off if no one is in the room.

HIGH-EFFICIENCY LIGHT FIXTURES

BUILDING MATERIALS
Eco-friendly building materials reduce emissions.

RAINWATER UTILIZATION SYSTEMS

SMART HEATING AND COOLING SYSTEMS

READING COMPREHENSION

A. Choose the best answer for each question.

GIST
1. What would be the best alternative title for this reading?

    a. How Oil Has Changed Dubai   c. Dubai's Economic Future

    b. The Costs of Green Living   d. Building a Sustainable City

PURPOSE
2. Why does the writer start the passage by describing a ski resort?

    a. to demonstrate the problems of living near a desert

    b. to describe an expensive and unsuccessful building project

    c. to give an example of how Dubai is a wealthy modern city

    d. to provide a warning of what Dubai might be like in the future

VOCABULARY
3. The word *striking* in paragraph D is closest in meaning to _____.

    a. distinctive   c. isolated

    b. massive   d. uniform

DETAIL
4. Which feature of "green buildings" is NOT specifically mentioned by the writer in relation to Dubai's Sustainable City?

    a. use of energy-efficient lights

    b. storage of rainwater underground

    c. placement of solar panels on rooftops

    d. arrangement of houses to allow natural cooling

REFERENCE
5. At the beginning of the third sentence in paragraph F, *It* refers to _____.

    a. Dubai's government   c. the Sustainable City

    b. solar energy production   d. the indoor ski resort

SUMMARIZING
MAIN IDEAS

Review this
skill in Unit 2B

B. Match each paragraph from the reading (A–F) with the best description. One description is extra.

1. Paragraph A _____

2. Paragraph B _____

3. Paragraph C _____

4. Paragraph D _____

5. Paragraph E _____

6. Paragraph F _____

    a. Dubai's plans for the next few decades

    b. A green community at the edge of the desert

    c. An unlikely tourist attraction in a very hot environment

    d. A change in how some people perceive sustainable communities

    e. Dubai's economic development before the discovery of oil

    f. How Dubai's rapid growth led to benefits and environmental problems

    g. How Dubai's energy, buildings, and transportation have become greener

Identifying an Author's Opinion

Even if an author does not state their opinion explicitly, it may be possible to infer how they feel about a topic or issue from the language used. As you read, take note of any positive or negative words—particularly adjectives—or phrases to determine if the text has a more positive or negative tone. This helps give you an idea of the author's opinion.

IDENTIFYING
OPINION

A. Read the text below. Underline positive words and circle negative words. Do you think the author's tone is positive or negative? What is the author's overall opinion about coal? Discuss your ideas with a partner.

Formed deep underground, coal is a carbon-rich black rock that remains a vital energy source worldwide. It is abundant and relatively inexpensive to extract. But coal is dirty and dangerous.

Coal poses grave risks to human health. It has been linked to deadly diseases such as cancer and heart disease. Coal-burning power stations are recklessly releasing a toxic ash that ends up polluting our drinking water. To continue to rely so much on coal for our energy is foolhardy and irresponsible.

IDENTIFYING
OPINION

B. Look back at paragraphs C, D, and F of the reading passage. Is the author's tone more positive or negative? Find and underline the words that support your claim. Overall, what is the author's opinion about Dubai?

CRITICAL THINKING Applying Ideas

▶ Make a list of things that Dubai is doing to reduce its ecological footprint.

▶ Which of the things in your list is your community or country doing? Discuss your ideas with a partner.

Coal mining at Savage Energy Terminal in Utah, USA

COMPLETION **A.** Complete the information with words from the box. Four words are extra.

comprehensive	cooling	distributed	efficiency	emissions
regulation	resident	sustainable	unrealistic	wealthy

Florida's new town of Babcock Ranch may be the town of the future. Property developer Syd Kitson is creating a place that is almost completely ¹_____—one powered solely by the sun. Future ²_____ will live in high-tech homes where everything is powered by over 300,000 solar panels. To move around the town, people will ride in a solar-powered self-driving shuttle bus that produces zero ³_____. Of course, cloudy days reduce the ⁴_____ of the solar panels, however, meaning that the town may have to use regular electricity at times.

Kitson anticipates a town of 50,000 people by 2040. And the town will not just be for ⁵_____ people. Home prices are only slightly higher than the state average. Although some people suggest it's ⁶_____ to think Babcock Ranch can be a model for future towns, Kitson is more optimistic. "We want to prove that something like this can work economically so that others will do it."

DEFINITIONS **B.** Match the definitions (1–8) to words from the box in **A**. Two words are not needed.

1. making less warm   _____
2. including everything   _____
3. spread evenly throughout an area   _____
4. not sensible or practical   _____
5. a rule set forth by an authority or agency _____
6. ability to perform well with very little waste _____
7. pollution released into the air   _____
8. able to be maintained   _____

WORD FORMS **C.** Many words have more than one form. Complete the chart with the correct forms.

Verb	Noun	Adjective
		ecological
	emission	
distribute		
	efficiency	
	sustainability	sustainable
reside	resident	

∨ Scientists and engineers are finding new ways to generate energy from the ocean.

WAVE POWER

BEFORE YOU WATCH

MATCHING **A. Match the captions (1–4) to the items in the picture.**

1. *Snakes*—Waves move the colorful "snake" up and down, moving the water **pumps** inside.
2. *Kites*—Small underwater **turbines**—attached in triangles to the ocean floor—generate power.
3. *Fans*—The changing **tides** move the underwater blades, which act in a similar way to wind turbines.
4. *Paddles*—Floating paddles move up and down, pushing water through high-pressure **pipes** that drive an onshore turbine.

MATCHING **B. Match the words in bold in A with their definitions.**

1. _____ long, hollow tubes for carrying water, gas, steam, etc.
2. _____ devices that force air, water, gas, etc., in or out of something
3. _____ engines that have parts that turn with the help of water, wind, etc.
4. _____ the alternating rising and falling of the ocean that occurs each day

MAIN IDEA **A.** Check (✓) the main idea of the video.

　　　1. _____ A new invention holds great promise as an energy source.

　　　2. _____ Several competing companies are finding ways to get energy from the ocean.

　　　3. _____ It's becoming easier to generate power from waves, but it's still too expensive.

COMPLETION **B.** Watch the video again. Complete the facts about Pelamis with the words and phrases in the box. Two items are extra.

| high pressure | monster | Portugal | Scotland |
| sea snake | temperatures | weather conditions | |

- Pelamis is named after a tropical [1]_____.
- Water pumps force water through a motor under [2]_____ generating electricity.
- Pelamis was first tested in a lab where wave stimulators recreated different [3]_____.
- Scale models were created, and the first test of a prototype was done in [4]_____.
- It was first used commercially in [5]_____, beginning in 2008.

CRITICAL THINKING Synthesizing   Discuss these questions with a partner.

▶ What are some possible disadvantages of generating power from ocean waves and tides?

▶ From what you have learned in this unit, which do you think has the most potential—solar, wind, nuclear, or wave power?

VOCABULARY REVIEW

Do you remember the meanings of these words? Check (✓) the ones you know. Look back at the unit and review any words you're not sure of.

Reading A

☐ capacity*　　☐ decline*　　☐ dispose*　　☐ eliminate*　　☐ equivalent*

☐ guarantee*　　☐ protest　　☐ steep　　☐ substitute*　　☐ utilize*

Reading B

☐ comprehensive　　☐ cooling　　☐ distribute*　　☐ efficiency　　☐ emissions

☐ regulation*　　☐ resident*　　☐ sustainable*　　☐ unrealistic　　☐ wealthy

* Academic Word List

8

EPIC ENGINEERING

Capital Gate, also called the Leaning Tower of Abu Dhabi, is one of the most distinctive buildings in the United Arab Emirates.

WARM UP

Discuss these questions with a partner.

1. What are some of the world's most impressive buildings or structures?

2. What are some impressive feats of engineering in your country? How would you describe them?

BEFORE YOU READ

SCANNING   **A.** Study the map on page 125. Discuss these questions with a partner.

      1. When was the Grand Canal's golden age?

      2. What was the canal used for?

      3. What were its northernmost and southernmost cities?

      4. How long was the Grand Canal during its golden age?

PREDICTING   **B.** Why do you think the Grand Canal has been important for China? Share your ideas with a partner. Then read the passage to check your ideas.

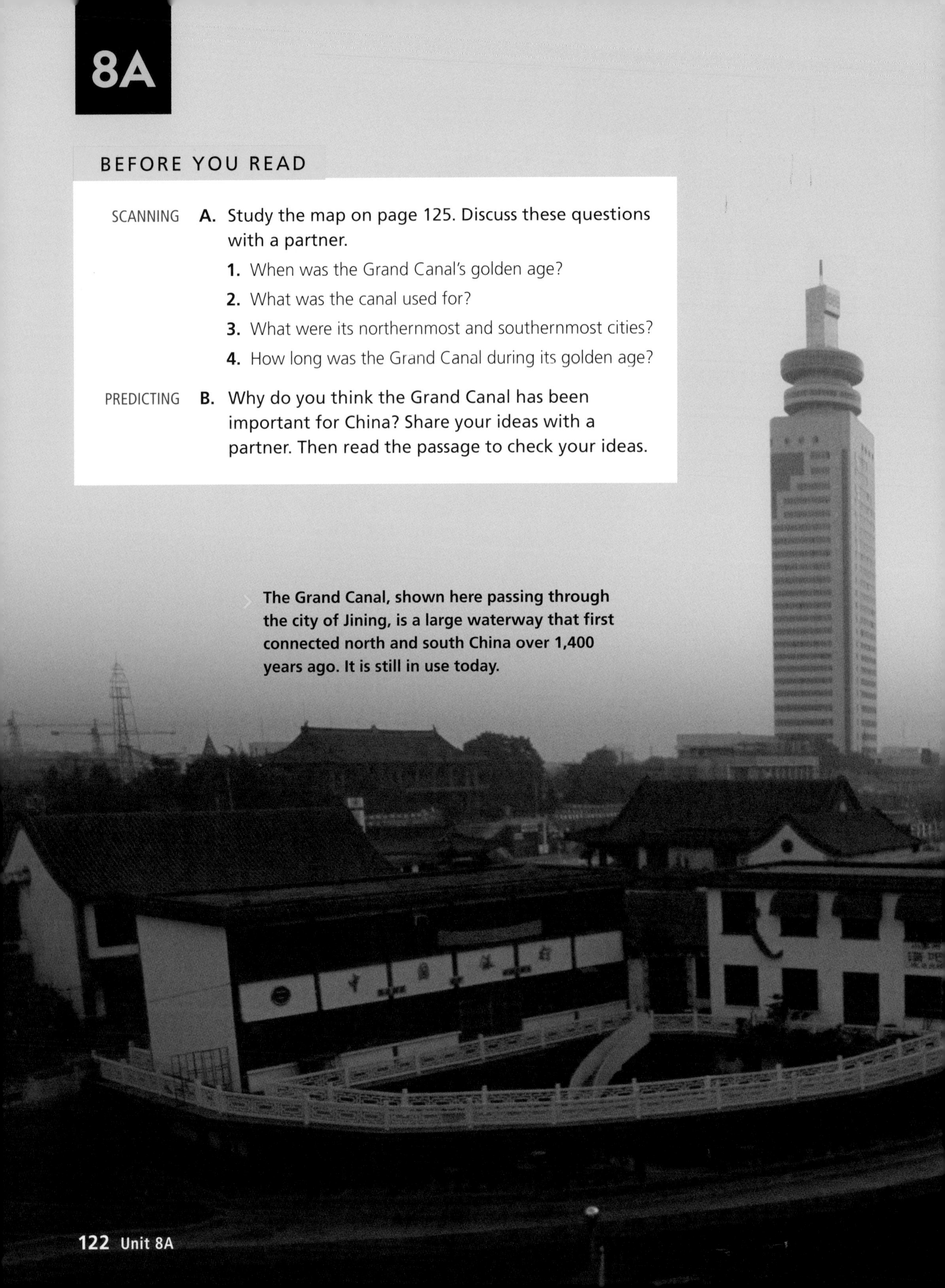

> **The Grand Canal, shown here passing through the city of Jining, is a large waterway that first connected north and south China over 1,400 years ago. It is still in use today.**

CHINA'S GRAND CANAL

A For centuries, the power of Chinese emperors rose and fell with their control of the Grand Canal. Today, this waterway is shorter than it once was, but it is still the longest man-made river in the world. Importantly, the Grand Canal continues to provide a vital cultural and economic link for modern China.

Construction Begins

B The original canal system began around the year 605. China's Emperor Yang realized that he needed a better way to feed his army. Specifically, he needed a way to move food quickly from China's southern rice-growing region to the country's north. So, the emperor ordered the construction of the first section of the Grand Canal, connecting existing canals, lakes, and rivers. An estimated one million people—mostly farmers—worked on the construction, which took six years.

C Over the next 500 years, the canal's importance grew. However, by 1127, parts had begun to deteriorate.[1] In 1279, Kublai Khan began to **repair** and build new parts of the canal. This **renovation** created a more direct north–south route to and from Beijing. Future rulers continued to expand and improve the waterway, and it eventually became a vital national lifeline.

D In addition to moving rice around China, the Grand Canal was an important cultural conduit.[2] Soldiers, merchants, and artists **transported** ideas, **regional** foods, and cultural practices from one part of China to another. According to legend, this is how

---

1 If something **deteriorates**, it gets worse in some way.
2 A **conduit** is something that connects two or more people, places, or things.

Beijing **acquired** two of its best-known trademarks. Peking[3] duck, a dish from Shandong Province, and the Peking opera, from Anhui and Hubei regions, were both brought north via the canal.

The Modern Canal

E For more than a thousand years, goods have been transported along the Grand Canal. Even today, the country's watery highway plays an important economic role in China. Boats continue to carry tons of coal, food, and other goods to points between Hangzhou and Jining—now the northernmost city the canal reaches. In addition, local governments—eager to increase tourism and real estate[4] development—are beautifying areas along the canal.

F This development comes at a price, though. In Yangzhou, the city has torn down almost all of the older canal-side buildings. Farther south in the cities of Zhenjiang, Wuxi, and Hangzhou, the situation is similar. In Hangzhou, for example, almost all of the ancient buildings have been **demolished**. "Traditionally we talk about 18 main cities on the Grand Canal, and each had something unique and special about it," explains Zhou Xinhua, the **former** vice director of the Grand Canal museum in Hangzhou. "But now many of these cities are all the same: a thousand people with one face."

G In 2005, a group of **citizens** proposed that the historic Grand Canal be made a UNESCO World Heritage Site. This status would protect both the waterway and the architecture around it. "Every generation wants the next generation to understand it, to look at its **monuments**," said Zhu Bingren, an artist who cowrote this **proposal**. UNESCO status was officially granted in 2014. The hope now is that the Grand Canal—one of the world's great engineering accomplishments—will continue to link north and south China for centuries to come.

---

3 **Peking** is the former name for Beijing.
4 **Real estate** is property in the form of land and buildings.

A boat travels down the Beijing-Hangzhou Grand Canal.

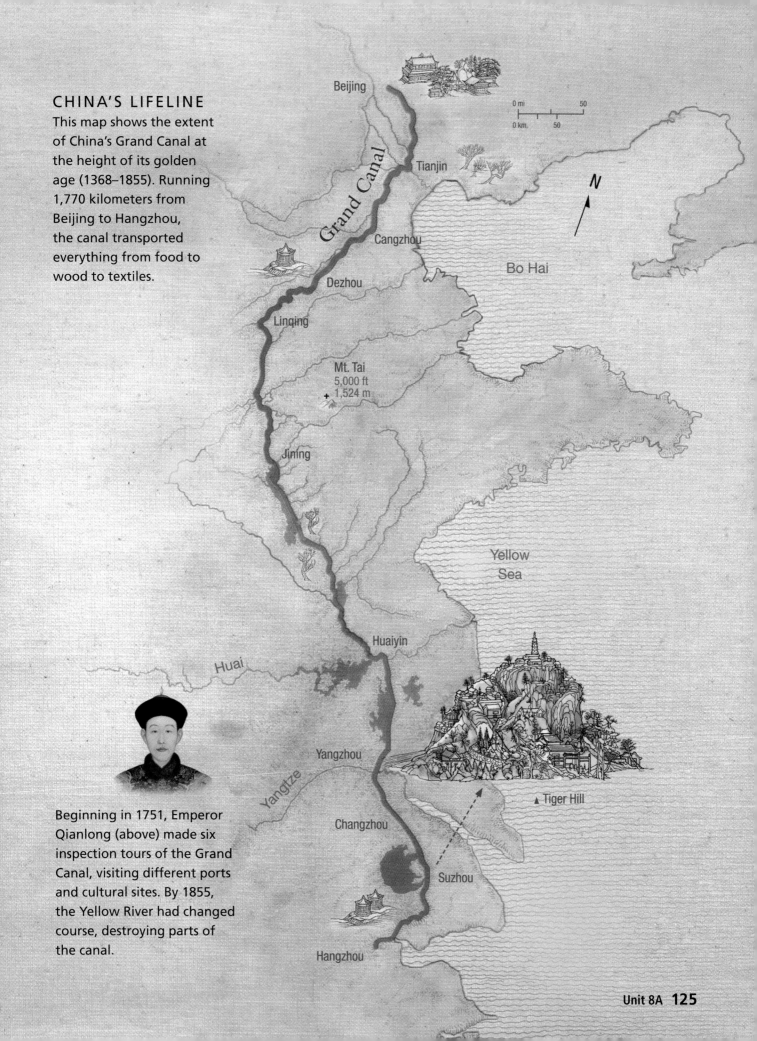

CHINA'S LIFELINE

This map shows the extent of China's Grand Canal at the height of its golden age (1368–1855). Running 1,770 kilometers from Beijing to Hangzhou, the canal transported everything from food to wood to textiles.

Beginning in 1751, Emperor Qianlong (above) made six inspection tours of the Grand Canal, visiting different ports and cultural sites. By 1855, the Yellow River had changed course, destroying parts of the canal.

Beijing

Grand Canal

Tianjin

Cangzhou

Bo Hai

Dezhou

Linqing

Mt. Tai
5,000 ft
1,524 m

Jining

Yellow Sea

Huaiyin

Huai

Yangzhou

Yangtze

Tiger Hill

Changzhou

Suzhou

Hangzhou

0 mi   50
0 km   50

N

A. Choose the best answer for each question.

DETAIL

1. Why was the Grand Canal originally built?

a. to allow the army to move quickly from the north to the south
b. to transport food from the southern regions of China to the north
c. to enable more people to visit remote parts of China
d. to promote the cultural and traditional diversity of south China

DETAIL

2. What is NOT true about the Grand Canal?

a. It originally took six years to complete its construction.
b. Even today, it is the longest man-made river in the world.
c. Around a million people worked on the first part of the canal.
d. It allowed Peking duck and the Peking opera to spread to southern China.

MAIN IDEA

3. What would be the best alternative heading for paragraph D?

a. Renewed Importance
b. Cultural Connections
c. The Army's Highway
d. The Origins of the Peking Opera

PARAPHRASE

4. Which of the following is closest in meaning to *This development comes at a price, though.* (paragraph F)?

a. But developing the canal involves spending a lot of money.
b. But even after spending money, people dislike the development.
c. But developing it is a lot more expensive than one can imagine.
d. But there are some negative consequences to this development.

COHESION

5. The following sentence would best be placed at the end of which paragraph? *The city of Yangzhou, for example, has created a beautiful park near its waterfront.*

a. A   b. D   c. E   d. G

TIMELINE

B. Add the events (a–f) to complete the timeline of the Grand Canal.

a. End of the canal's golden age.
b. New parts of the canal built.
c. Construction of the Grand Canal begins.
d. Canal becomes a World Heritage Site.
e. Emperor Qianlong first tours the canal.
f. Construction is completed.

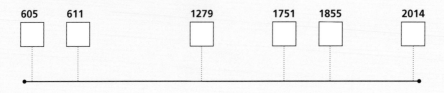

Understanding Vocabulary: Compound Words

One type of word you may come across in a reading passage is a compound word. A compound word is made when two (or more) words are put together to create a new word. To understand its meaning, look at the meaning of the individual words. Compound words can be a single word (e.g., *waterway*), two words (e.g., *real estate*), or two words linked by a hyphen (e.g., *man-made*).

DEFINITIONS **A.** Find and underline the compound words in paragraphs C and D. Then write them next to their definitions (1–4).

1. _____: most widely recognized

2. _____: a river or canal that can be used for travel

3. _____: special features that a person or place is known for

4. _____: something that provides help or support needed for survival

COMPLETION **B.** Complete the information with compound words. Use one word from box A and one word from box B for each item (1–6). Use a dictionary to help you.

A		
day	high	life
man	well	with

B		
light	known	made
out	time	trip

In addition to the Grand Canal, China is ¹_____ for another ²_____ wonder—the Great Wall. China's first emperor wanted a wall for protection. ³_____ a wall, his country was vulnerable to attack from the north. Construction began during the first emperor's ⁴_____, but work continued for many hundreds of years after his death. Each emperor added to the wall to protect his power. Construction continued until the wall was thousands of kilometers long. Today, the Great Wall still stands. It can be easily visited on a ⁵_____ from Beijing and is a ⁶_____ for many locals and international visitors.

⌃ **A section of the Great Wall at Badaling, near Beijing**

CRITICAL THINKING Interpreting Meaning

▶ According to Zhou Xinhua, what was "special and unique" about the cities along the Grand Canal?

▶ What does Zhou Xinhua mean when he says the cities are now like "a thousand people with one face"?

COMPLETION **A. Complete the information. Circle the correct words.**

The 77-kilometer Panama Canal is one of the world's greatest engineering achievements. There were ¹**monuments / proposals** for a canal as early as the 16th century, but it wasn't until 1881 when the French started to build a canal.

The United States ²**repaired / acquired** the canal project in the early 19th century for $40 million. Construction was completed in 1914 under the supervision of chief engineer George Washington Goethals. A ³**citizen / monument** honoring Goethals stands today in Panama City.

A recent $5.2 billion ⁴**renovation / citizen** and expansion project allows much larger ships to pass through the canal. This has led to a sharp increase in the amount of goods that can be ⁵**demolished / transported** through the canal. Today, nearly 14,000 ships pass through the Panama Canal every year.

∧ **Aerial view of the Panama Canal**

DEFINITIONS **B. Complete each sentence with the correct answer.**

1. If you **repair** a phone, you _____ it.
   a. clean   b. fix

2. A **former** president is a _____ president.
   a. past   b. future

3. A **citizen** of a country _____ the legal rights of that country.
   a. has   b. does not have

4. If you **demolish** a building, you _____ it.
   a. build   b. destroy

5. A **regional** language is spoken by most people in _____ a country.
   a. a particular area of   b. all parts of

WORD LINK **C. The word renovation contains the root *nov* which means "new." Complete the sentences with the correct word from the box. There is one extra word.**

innovate	novelty	novice	renovated

1. Companies that _____ do better than businesses that don't invest in new products and ideas.

2. Because of rust and structural issues, New York's iconic Statue of Liberty was _____ in the 1980s.

3. Cell phones were a _____ item in 1983. Now, almost everyone has one.

BEFORE YOU READ

DISCUSSION **A.** Read the caption below. Then answer the questions with a partner.

    1. Many Peruvians are happy about the construction of the Transoceanic Highway. Why do you think this is?

    2. What concerns might environmentalists have about the highway?

SCANNING **B.** Scan the reading on the next two pages, and underline answers to the two questions above. Then read the passage closely to check your ideas.

∨ This road is part of the 2,600-kilometer Transoceanic Highway. The highway stretches from the Pacific Ocean in Peru and connects with Brazil's already existing highways, which extend to the Atlantic Ocean.

^ Sunset over the Amazon rain forest, Madre de Dios, Peru

A **A new road that connects the Pacific with the Atlantic could bring riches—and environmental ruin.**

B Mary Luz Guerra remembers a trip she took in 2003 from the city of Cusco, high in the Peruvian Andes, to her home in Puerto Maldonado, a city in the Amazon rain forest. By plane, this 320-kilometer journey would have taken only 37 minutes, but Mary had traveled by truck along narrow mountain roads, across rushing rivers, and through **dense** jungle. It took her three days to reach home. During the long trip, she remembers thinking, "I can't wait till they build that highway!" Almost 10 years after that long journey, Mary's wish came true.

Bridging a Continent

C In early 2012, the Transoceanic Highway opened to public vehicles for the first time. A dream of Peru's political leaders since the 1950s, work on the vast network of roads and bridges began in 2006 and was completed in 2011. Today, the east–west passageway

spans 2,600 kilometers. From Peru's Pacific Ocean coastline, it continues across the Andes Mountains and through a large part of Peru's Amazon rain forest. It then travels into Brazil, where it connects with a network of existing highways to the Atlantic.

D The Transoceanic Highway has been celebrated as one of South America's greatest engineering feats, and supporters say it will greatly improve people's lives. Until recently, travel between the cities of Cusco and Puerto Maldonado in Peru took days by bus or truck—as Mary's story **illustrates**—and drivers had to use narrow, **partially** unpaved[1] mountain roads. Now the trip only takes a few hours, and is much safer.

Improving People's Lives

E In addition to making travel faster and easier, supporters say the highway will be good for business. There is **enormous** demand in North America and Asia for Brazilian and

---

1 If a road is **unpaved**, it is mostly dirt.

Peruvian products, including soybeans, beef, and gold. A number of companies in Cusco and Puerto Maldonado also sell wood to different corners of the world. Many of these companies transport their lumber[2] to the Pacific, where it travels by ship to other countries. Thanks to the highway, wood can now reach the Pacific in days; in the past, it could take a week or more. This lowers costs and allows the wood to reach customers sooner, and in better condition. In the long run, say many business owners, this will mean more profit.

F The highway will also open up areas of the Peruvian Amazon that were not **accessible** just a few years ago. This may increase activity in these areas and give people new places to live in and travel to. This, in turn, could mean more jobs and money for Peruvians.

---

2 **Lumber** is wood that has been cut into boards.
3 **Biodiversity** is the existence of a wide variety of living things (plants, animals, insects, etc.) in a certain place.
4 If something is **pristine**, it is in its original condition or is unspoiled.

Environmental Challenges

G Despite the highway's many potential benefits, environmentalists are concerned. The Transoceanic passes directly through a large part of the Amazon rain forest, in the state of Madre de Dios in Peru. According to a Peruvian government study, the forested area in the western mountains of this state has the greatest biodiversity[3] of any place on Earth, and until recently, large parts of the forest were in pristine[4] condition. As more people move into the region, environmentalists worry about the **impact** this will have on the Amazon's plants and animals, many of which are found nowhere else.

H Shortly after the highway opened, large numbers of people began coming into Puerto Maldonado from all over Peru—and the world—to mine gold. There's a lot of money to be made in mining, as well as in farming, says environmental photographer Gabby Salazar. "I think we're going to see a big increase in farming," she says. "Right across the **border** in Brazil, you see soybean farms all over the place." Studies show that 95 percent of the deforestation[5] of the Brazilian Amazon **occurs** within 50 kilometers of a highway, and environmentalists like Salazar are concerned that the same thing is happening in Peru. "It's having an impact on the environment," she explains. "It's having an impact on the people as well."

I Faced with these risks, many Peruvians talk about the importance of being **practical**. "In rural[6] Peru, a lot of people are living in poverty, so it's very difficult to say don't build the highway," explains Roger Mustalish, president of the Amazon Center for Environmental Education and Research. "But every time you see a road like this going through, you soon see major changes." Will these changes be mostly positive or negative? Many Peruvians are hopeful, but only time will tell.

---

5 **Deforestation** is the destruction or cutting down of all the trees in an area.
6 **Rural** places are in the country, far away from cities.

A. Choose the best answer for each question.

GIST

1. What is the reading mainly about?

    a. a new highway's likely impact on Peru's environment and people

    b. how the Brazilian government helped to build a new highway

    c. a new development that is resulting in mining and farming jobs

    d. how the Amazon's biodiversity is being protected from development

DETAIL

2. What is true about the Transoceanic Highway?

    a. Its construction began in the 1950s.

    b. It helps connect the Pacific Ocean with Brazil.

    c. It was opened to the public in 2006.

    d. It begins at the Atlantic Ocean.

VOCABULARY

3. The phrase *In the long run* (paragraph E) could be replaced by _____.

    a. on the other hand   c. as expected

    b. eventually   d. optimistically

DETAIL

4. Which of the following concerns does the reading specifically mention?

    a. Increased mining will lead to soil erosion.

    b. Farming will lead to an increase in water pollution.

    c. The highway will have an impact on the area's biodiversity.

    d. The cities along the highway will become overpopulated.

MAIN IDEA

5. What would be the best heading for paragraph I?

    a. A Positive Future?   c. Completing the Highway

    b. Say No to Highways   d. An End to Poverty

PROS AND CONS

B. Use words from the reading passage to complete the chart. Use one word for each item.

Review This Skill in Unit 6A

How the highway may help	How the highway may harm
• 1_____, safer, easier to travel; good for business	• crosses area with the greatest 4_____ of anywhere on Earth
• gives people new areas to 2_____ in and travel to	• crosses area in 5_____ condition; has impact on plants, animals, people
• more 3_____ and more money for locals	• leads to deforestation from mining and 6_____

Inferring Information (1)

Not all details are stated directly in a text. Often a reader will need to make inferences—to look at other details and references to work out what is being stated. Look at the example.

The wildfires severely affected Oakland and other cities in California.

We know that Oakland is in California because it can be inferred from the phrase "other cities in California."

A successful reader can not only infer facts, but also infer the author's feelings or opinions.

INFERRING **A.** **Look back at the reading passage. Can you infer the information below from the information given in the passage? Circle Yes or No.**

1. Mary Luz Guerra was a young girl when she first traveled to Puerto Maldonado. (paragraph B)   **Yes No**

2. The Peruvian government built the Transoceanic Highway. (paragraph C)   **Yes No**

3. The old road from Cusco to Puerto Maldonado was dangerous. (paragraph D)   **Yes No**

4 Peruvian products are popular in Europe. (paragraph E)   **Yes No**

5. The rain forest in Madre de Dios is no longer pristine. (paragraph G)   **Yes No**

INFERRING **B.** **Look back again at the passage. Note answers to the questions. Then discuss with a partner how you inferred the answers.**

1. How do you think Mary Luz Guerra feels about the old highway?

_____

2. Do you think the author feels positive, negative, or neutral about the Transoceanic Highway? Why?

_____

_____

CRITICAL THINKING Synthesizing Ideas

▶ List ways in which China's Grand Canal and Peru's Transoceanic Highway are similar. Consider the following areas:

    Construction   **Purpose**   **Benefits**   **Costs**

_____

_____

▶ Do you think the Transoceanic Highway will be as successful as the Grand Canal? Will it last as long? Explain your answers to a partner.

VOCABULARY PRACTICE

COMPLETION **A.** Complete the information. Circle the correct words.

∧ **The Gotthard Railway has the world's longest railway tunnel.**

For two decades, engineers worked deep under the Swiss Alps, building a(n) [1]**enormous / partial** tunnel. When it opened in 2016, the Gotthard Base Tunnel became the world's longest and deepest railway tunnel. As a symbol of cross-[2]**border / accessible** cooperation, the tunnel allows trains to travel under the Alps from Germany to Italy at 250 kilometers per hour. In the last few decades, a huge number of trucks crossing the Alps has had an enormous [3]**illustrating / impact** on the environment. The new tunnel provides a [4]**practical / dense** solution to this problem. Goods can now be transported by train without [5]**occurring / ruining** the beautiful mountain landscape.

B. Use the correct form of words in **A** to complete the definitions. Five words are not needed.

1. A(n) _____ jungle has many plants in it.
2. If something _____, it exists or happens.
3. When a project is _____ completed, it is not completely finished.
4. If something is _____, it is easy or possible to reach.
5. If something _____ an idea, it serves as an example.

COLLOCATIONS **C.** The nouns in the box are often used with **dense**. Add them to the correct sentences. One word is extra.

crowds	fog	layers	network	population

1. Computers from the 1960s were very large, and included a dense _____ of wires and cables.
2. Dense _____ can make driving slow and dangerous.
3. The atmosphere on Jupiter is made up of several dense _____ of swirling, toxic clouds.
4. Recent research suggests people like to keep 75 cm apart in public settings—this is hard to do in dense _____ .

Rain forest exhibit at the California
Academy of Sciences

BUILDING A
RAIN FOREST

BEFORE YOU WATCH

DEFINITIONS **A.** Read the description of a "Green Museum." Match the words in **bold** to the definitions below.

Inside a giant glass **dome**, the rain forest exhibit at the California Academy of Sciences is an impressive sight. Guests walk up a spiral **ramp** inside the dome, all the way up through the trees to the **canopy**, to parts of the tree that would normally be inaccessible. Then they ride a glass elevator all the way down to a **tunnel** under the rain forest, where they can see the marine animals in the **aquarium**.

1. A(n) _____ is a roofing structure that is in the circular shape similar to an upside-down bowl.

2. A(n) _____ is a building that houses live sea creatures.

3. The _____ is the highest layer of tree branches in a forest.

4. A(n) _____ is an underground passage.

5. A(n) _____ is a short road or pathway that connects two levels.

GIST **A.** Watch the video. Check (✓) the statements that are true, according to the video.

☐ **1.** Chris Andrews helped to create the indoor rain forest.

☐ **2.** The atmosphere in the forest is kept cool and dry.

☐ **3.** Visitors can also visit the world's deepest coral reef tank.

☐ **4.** The aquarium exhibit contains thousands of fish.

MULTIPLE CHOICE **B.** Choose the best answer for each question.

1. What does Chris Andrews say about the rain forest exhibit?

a. There will be two of every animal.   b. It will feel and smell like a real rain forest.

c. It will be as good as replacing nature.

2. Where does the aquarium get its water from?

a. the city water supply   b. a nearby river   c. the Pacific Ocean

3. Who is Diego?

a. a turtle   b. the first visitor   c. a museum employee

CRITICAL THINKING Applying Ideas   Work in a group. Imagine you want to create a new museum or other attraction to bring in visitors to your local town or area. Discuss the following questions.

What would the building look like?   Where would it be located?

What features would it include?   Why would it be special?

Draw a plan of your attraction and label the important features. Share your ideas with another group.

VOCABULARY REVIEW

Do you remember the meanings of these words? Check (✓) the ones you know. Look back at the unit and review any words you're not sure of.

Reading A

☐ acquire*   ☐ citizen   ☐ demolish   ☐ former   ☐ monument

☐ proposal   ☐ regional   ☐ renovation   ☐ repair   ☐ transport*

Reading B

☐ accessible*   ☐ border   ☐ dense   ☐ enormous*   ☐ illustrate*

☐ impact*   ☐ occur*   ☐ partially   ☐ practical   ☐ ruin

* Academic Word List

9

HIGH-TECH SOLUTIONS

An augmented reality display provides a driver with up-to-date traffic and weather information.

Discuss these questions with a partner.

1. What types of new technology have you seen in the past 10 years?

2. Have any of these types of technology been helpful to you? In what ways?

137

BEFORE YOU READ

DISCUSSION **A.** Read the caption below. What could be some other uses of VR? Discuss with a partner.

PREDICTING **B.** How might VR be used in the areas below? Note your ideas. Then read the passage to learn more.

- Training athletes
- Helping with business meetings
- Raising environmental awareness

> A patient experiences a Virtual Reality (VR) therapy session in Marseille, France. VR is an interactive simulation of a realistic environment using computer-generated sounds and visuals.

THE POWER OF VIRTUAL REALITY

A People have talked about the possibilities of virtual reality since the mid-1990s. In this interview, Jeremy Bailenson—director of the Virtual Human Interactive Lab at Stanford University—explains how these possibilities are now becoming real.

Interviewer: What's the difference between watching a video and wearing a VR headset?

B **JB:** The difference is what psychologists call "embodied cognition." That is, we learn by doing. For a lot of the most important learning events in your life, you actually did something—you walked somewhere or felt something. Similarly, Virtual Reality is active, not **passive**. You learn in ways that people have been learning for hundreds of thousands of years: by having an experience.

C Our lab studies have shown that, in general, the brain tends to **treat** a VR event in a similar way to an **actual** event. So there's a difference between performing an event in a traditional video game and doing it inside VR.

Interviewer: You've said that VR can help athletes. What's an example of that?

D **JB:** We **demonstrated** in the 2014 NFL[1] season that VR could help quarterbacks[2] by improving their decision-making accuracy and reducing their reaction times. Carson Palmer is one of the earliest adopters. VR gave him a tool he could use to learn the plays[3] better. Carson had a system in his home. For just a couple minutes a day, after he'd wake up, he'd **go over** his plays and mentally practice what he was going to do. It was as though he were actually on the field. But he was in his living room, getting extra practice.

E Since then, VR has been used by teams across many sports. The German national soccer team, among others, uses it in their practice quite often.

---

1 The **NFL** (National Football League) is a professional American football league.
2 In American football, the **quarterback** is a player who directs a team's attack.
3 In sports, a **play** is a planned action that happens in a game.

> A video gamer tries a wireless VR headset at the 2019 Consumer Electronics Show in Las Vegas.

Interviewer: Explain how VR avatars[4] can improve video conferencing.

F **JB:** Video conferencing is good for some activities. But it's not good for an important meeting where intense decisions have to be made. One reason is the eye contact problem. If you look at the camera on the top of your laptop, you don't see the other person. **Conversely**, if you look at the other person's image on your screen, you're not looking at the camera.

G Psychologists have shown that *very* small changes in things like eye contact, body space, or posture **alter** the way conversations flow. With VR avatars, you can control things like body position and eye contact in a way you can't do with video **conferences**.

Interviewer: You have said that VR can help save the planet. How can VR raise awareness of environmental issues?

H **JB:** One example is an experiment on the island of Ischia, in Italy. Ischia is a marine site that scientists have been studying for decades. Carbon dioxide is destroying its coral and degrading[5] the food web.[6] I can't bring the entire world to Ischia to show how CO_2 degrades ecosystems. But with VR, I can bring Ischia to *people*.

---

4 An **avatar** is a 3-D image of a person. In a VR conference, each participant's avatar appears on screen in the same room.

5 If a chemical **degrades** something, it causes it to break down and deteriorate.

6 A **food web** is a combination of the individual food chains in a community.

So, we produced a seven-minute journey that shows how all the oceans will look in about 50 years, based on this one site in Ischia. Using this VR model, people **get to** be scientists. They explore the effects of CO_2 on various species in the ecosystem, and learn by *doing*.

Interviewer: What about the **downsides** of VR—for example, using it to create violent video games?

JB: The way I think of VR is that we should use it for things that we can't do in the real world. You should use VR to go to the moon or try becoming someone else. But you *shouldn't* do things that you *wouldn't* do in the real world.

Interviewer: In your opinion, will VR change how we interact with other people in the real world?

JB: VR is a tool, just like any other media. But it has a different impact on how we perceive information. That's because you're using your body and it's completely immersive. It's a big jump in the history of media. But I don't think it's going to change who people are. I think we will continue to be the same humans that we have been on the planet for quite some time. And I, for one, am glad of that.

The interview was edited for length and clarity.

A soccer goalkeeper trains using a Virtual Reality headset.

A. Choose the best answer for each question.

GIST

1. What would be the best alternative title for this passage?

    a. How VR Brings Us All Together
    b. The Future of VR Gaming
    c. VR: A Useful Tool for the 21st Century
    d. Saving the Planet with VR

INFERENCE

2. Which of these is NOT an example of embodied cognition?

    a. watching a soccer game on TV
    b. cooking a meal using a recipe
    c. completing a crossword puzzle
    d. playing a musical instrument

⌃ **Sales of VR headsets are projected to be over 120 million in 2022.**

MAIN IDEA

3. What is the purpose of the Ischia VR model?

    a. to propose a new way of saving sea life near Ischia
    b. to recreate what the climate in Italy was like in the past
    c. to show how oceans are being damaged by climate change
    d. to explain how pollution from Ischia is affecting other areas

VOCABULARY

4. Which of the following is closest in meaning to *adopters* in paragraph D?

    a. users   c. athletes
    b. inventors   d. quarterbacks

PARAPHRASE

5. What is Bailenson's main point in the final paragraph (K)?

    a. Although VR technology is improving, other media will still be important.
    b. VR is a major change, but it will not fundamentally change who we are.
    c. It will take several years before people's lives are really affected by VR.
    d. VR's impact is significant, but many people in the world will not notice it.

SHORT ANSWER

B. Write short answers. Use no more than three words from the reading passage for each answer.

1. According to Bailenson, how do people learn best? _____

2. In what other way did VR help American football players, in addition to improving decision-making? _____

3. In what other way can VR avatars improve video conferencing, in addition to body posture and space? _____

4. What does the Ischia VR model allow people to be? _____

5. How is VR similar to other types of media? _____

Applying Information from a Text

When you read a text, it is useful to consider how the writer's ideas might apply to other contexts. This can help you evaluate the usefulness of the writer's ideas and think about how well they transfer to other situations. When you apply information, you might predict what could happen in a similar situation, solve a problem using ideas from a text, or infer other information based on the writer's ideas.

IDENTIFYING
ADVANTAGES

A. Match the advantages of using VR (a–f) to each situation, according to the passage. One advantage is not stated in the text.

Advantages of using VR…

1. to help athletes:

_____ _____

2. to improve video conferencing:

_____

3. at the Ischia marine site:

_____ _____

People can…

a. have clearer interactions with others.

b. react to situations more quickly.

c. visualize the impact on an environment over time.

d. see a place they'd normally not be able to visit.

e. avoid dangerous or life-threatening situations.

f. practice the same action many times.

APPLYING
INFORMATION

B. Discuss these questions with a partner.

1. Aside from athletes, what other professions might benefit from VR? Consider people working in the following areas:

architecture   education   entertainment   health care   tourism

2. What other environmental problems might VR help people visualize better? How could VR help people explore the effects of these problems? Note down your ideas.

_____

_____

_____

CRITICAL THINKING Evaluating Pros and Cons

▶ What does the interviewer suggest is one possible downside to VR? Note it down.

_____

▶ What additional downsides to VR can you think of? Consider the areas below. Discuss your ideas with a partner.

health effects   social effects   financial effects

COMPLETION   **A.** Complete the paragraph with words or phrases from the box. One word is extra.

actual	alter	get to	going over	passive	treat

Virtual reality therapy (VRT) is a way to [1]_____ patients who suffer from psychological trauma.[1] As with traditional treatments, VRT helps patients visualize the traumatic event so that they can overcome it. Instead of lying down and just talking to a therapist, VRT patients take a less [2]_____ role: They use a VR headset to see, hear, and sometimes even smell the event. For example, a soldier can go back to a battlefield, or a firefighter can return to a burning building. In this way, patients [3]_____ experience a virtual version that is similar to the [4]_____ traumatic event. By [5]_____ the event virtually, patients are able to reduce their anxiety and make progress in their therapy.

⌃ **A patient uses VR to reduce her stress before surgery.**

1 **Psychological trauma** describes damage to the mind caused by a distressing situation.

WORDS IN CONTEXT   **B.** Complete each sentence. Choose the correct option.

1. The **downside** of something is the _____ aspect of it.
   a. positive   b. negative

2. At a **conference**, you are more likely to speak to _____.
   a. colleagues   b. family members

3. If you **demonstrate** a skill, you _____ it.
   a. show   b. hide

4. You use **conversely** to indicate an idea is _____ another idea.
   a. similar to   b. different from

WORD PARTS   **C.** The word **down** can be used to form certain compound words, such as **downside**. Complete the sentences with a word from the box. One word is not used.

download	downpour	downside	downsize	downturn

1. Places that don't get much rain can get flooded by a sudden _____.

2. For some people, a _____ of living in the suburbs is the long drive to work.

3. An increase in interest rates can cause a _____ in the housing market.

4. Once their children are grown up, some parents _____ to a smaller house.

BEFORE YOU READ

DISCUSSION
A. Look at the photo and read the caption. How do you think drones can be used in a positive way? Discuss with a partner, and note as many uses as you can think of.

_____

_____

SKIMMING
B. Skim the reading passage. Check (✓) the applications of drone technology that the writer describes. Then read the whole passage to check your ideas.

☐ surveying natural disasters ☐ locating threats to wildlife
☐ delivering medicines ☐ mapping oceans

> Some drones are used to photograph or film difficult-to-reach places; others are used to deliver items.

HIGH-FLYING
HELPERS

Drones—originally created as tools of war—are now performing important humanitarian and conservation tasks around the world.

In Malawi, drones are used to transport blood and other medical samples from villages to city hospitals.

Saving Lives

A Delivering **medical** supplies to hard-to-reach places has been an issue for years. Worldwide, more than two billion people lack access to essential life-saving supplies, such as blood and vaccines.[1] In the African nation of Rwanda, for example, several remote health clinics do not have **sufficient** quantities of blood and other healthcare products. As a result, many people die of treatable illnesses.

B A company called Zipline is trying to address this problem. It uses drones to transport medical supplies around Rwanda. In the past, it took hours for **packages** of medicines to reach some health clinics. However, a drone can now deliver medicine in 30 minutes. Thanks to this **rapid** healthcare service, fewer women suffer during childbirth and more children receive life-saving medicine.

C Drones are also assisting emergency organizations after natural disasters. In 2015, for example, a powerful cyclone destroyed thousands of buildings in the Pacific island nation of Vanuatu. Around 75,000 people lost their homes, and at least 15 died. After the storm, drones photographed the damage. These **surveys** helped emergency workers **assess** the situation quickly and answer important questions: Which areas were hardest hit? Were crops damaged? What roads were affected? Emergency workers used the data to create a detailed map of the affected area. They were then able to transport **aid** to the people who needed it most.

Eyes in the Sky

D Drones are also helping to protect vulnerable wildlife populations in parts of Africa and Asia. Every year, poachers[2] kill thousands of elephants, rhinos, and other endangered animals. To stop them, the environmental organization World Wildlife Fund (WWF) is using drones. "Drones help us see things we can't," says Colby Loucks, who works for the WWF. For example, they can show where poachers are hiding and if they are carrying weapons. Drones are particularly helpful at night, when poachers tend to be most active. Fitted with infrared video cameras, drones can easily identify people and animals in the dark. These drones are not only helpful, they are **affordable**. Drones with infrared cameras cost about $20,000 each—a fraction of the cost of other high-tech tools.

E As well as finding poachers, drones can be used to track animals. Scientists at Liverpool John Moores University plan to employ drones for an **ambitious** conservation project: documenting the world's wildlife. The long-term project will start with scientific surveys of animal populations. As the project expands, members of the public will be able to contribute by uploading their own drone footage.[3] Animal species can then be identified using special software. The project leader, biologist Serge Wich, predicts that drones—cheaper, more practical, and less dangerous than planes or helicopters—will become a widely used conservation tool. "I think we will have swarms of drones flying over forests," he predicts.

F Ironically, a tool originally created for **military** use is increasingly being used to save lives instead of taking them. Drones have the potential to provide solutions that will benefit both humans and animals, says photographer and environmentalist Kike Calvo. "There's nothing that can replace a good scientist," he says. But with the help of drones, "researchers are empowered to carry out projects they've never imagined before."

---

1 A **vaccine** is a medicine that prevents a dangerous disease.
2 **Poachers** are people who catch or kill animals illegally.
3 **Footage** of an event is the film that shows it.

A. Choose the best answer for each question.

GIST

1. What is the reading passage mainly about?

a. successes and failures of recent drone technology

b. how drone delivery times have improved in recent years

c. examples of positive uses of drone technology around the world

d. predictions for how drone technology will change in the future

∧ **A drone delivers a first-aid package.**

PURPOSE

2. What is the main purpose of Zipline's drones?

a. to transport medicines to people's homes

b. to identify clinics most in need of medicine

c. to deliver medical supplies after a disaster

d. to get supplies quickly to remote health clinics

DETAIL

3. After the 2015 Vanuatu disaster, what were drones primarily used for?

a. surveying storm damage

b. analyzing weather conditions

c. delivering medical supplies

d. sending emergency messages

MAIN IDEA

4. According to the passage, why are infrared drones especially useful?

a. They are silent and difficult to detect.

b. They can identify poachers at night.

c. They are cheaper than other types of drones.

d. They can be used near the ground and in the sky.

VOCABULARY

5. Which of these is closest in meaning to *swarms* in the last sentence of paragraph E?

a. new types   c. small groups

b. large numbers   d. different kinds

SHORT ANSWER

B. Write short answers. Use up to three words from the reading passage for each question.

1. What are two medical supplies that over two billion people do not have access to?

_____

2. About how long does it take to deliver a package to rural clinics using Zipline?

_____

3. What objects, belonging to poachers, are drones able to see?

_____

4. The John Moores project will eventually allow people to help by doing what?

_____

Recognizing Text Coherence

A reading passage is coherent when ideas flow together smoothly. Without coherence, a reader may have a difficult time understanding the main ideas and following the overall flow of a text. For a deeper understanding of a text, look for ways in which the writer connects his or her ideas. For example, notice how:

- key words and phrases (often nouns) are repeated to emphasize their importance
- synonyms for key terms show connections between sentences and paragraphs
- pronouns (*it, her*) and demonstratives (*that, those*) refer to previous ideas
- transitions (*However, In addition*) and conjunctions (*and, such as*) link ideas

ANALYZING **A. Look at the section "Saving Lives" in the reading passage. Answer the following questions.**

1. What key words or phrases related to *health* are used in paragraphs A and B?

   _____

2. What two synonyms for *far away* appear in paragraph A? _____

3. What transition is used to introduce a reason or cause in paragraph B? _____

4. What does *it* refer to in the last line of paragraph C? _____

ANALYZING **B. Look at the section "Eyes in the Skies." Choose the best answer for each question.**

1. What does *them* refer to in the third sentence of paragraph D?

   a. drones   b. elephants   c. poachers   d. the WWF

2. The author uses the transition *As well as* in paragraph E to give another example of how drones are _____.

   a. saving humans   c. helping conservationists
   b. tracking poachers   d. delivering medicines

3. In paragraph E, what example of *documenting* does the author NOT describe?

   a. doing surveys   c. interviewing people
   b. uploading drone footage   d. identifying species

4. In paragraph F, what does *a tool* refer to?

   a. photography   b. drones   c. conservation   d. special software

5. What does *them* refer to in paragraph F?

   a. tools   b. drones   c. military uses   d. lives

CRITICAL THINKING Applying Ideas   What other humanitarian or conservation tasks could drones be used for? List two ideas and share with a partner.

_____

_____

_____

COMPLETION **A.** Complete the information. Circle the correct words.

∧ **The 2-meter wide SmartBird drone was modeled after a herring gull.**

Quadcopters—the most popular type of drone today—work well to deliver [1]**medical / packages** and to [2]**aid / assess** storm damage. A quadcopter is practical and [3]**affordable / sufficient**, making it possible for even small organizations to buy. But it's a noisy machine compared to quieter, but more expensive, plane-like drones.

A(n) [4]**ambitious / rapid** new project aims to offer the best of both worlds: ornithopter drones. Ornithopters have flapping wings that can cross the sky quietly and efficiently. They can also take off and land in tight spaces. Drone builders hope to make ornithopter drones that work even more like birds. One day, drones could move as [5]**ambitiously / rapidly** as falcons—diving out of the sky at 320 kilometers per hour.

DEFINITIONS **B.** Complete the definitions. Circle the correct option.

1. If you give someone **aid**, you *help / move* them.
2. Someone who is **ambitious** is determined to *succeed / help*.
3. If you **survey** something, you examine it *in detail / slowly*.
4. If something is **sufficient**, it is *not enough / enough*.
5. The **military** mostly consists of *armed / unarmed* soldiers.
6. **Medical** supplies consist of items that improve people's *health / wealth*.

COLLOCATIONS **C.** The verbs in **bold** are often used before the noun **aid**. Circle the correct options.

1. Some homeless people **provide / receive** aid in the form of temporary shelter.
2. Many college students **depend on / withhold** financial aid to pay for their education.
3. An aid organization might **call for / suspend** aid operations if their emergency workers are in danger.
4. After it was hit by Hurricane Maria, officials in Puerto Rico **appealed for / extended** aid so they could rebuild.

DRONE DELIVERY

∧ A courier sends off a package using a delivery drone.

BEFORE YOU WATCH

DEFINITIONS **A.** Read the information. The words and phrases in **bold** appear in the video. Fill in the blanks to complete the definitions.

Matt Sweeny is the founder of a drone company called Flirtey. This little **startup** is competing with technology giants like Amazon and Google to provide a delivery service, **at a premium**, using drones that can **autonomously** deliver **over-the-counter** medicines and other products to customers' homes. Flirtey currently has a **head start** in the market, but whether it can succeed in the delivery business is yet to be seen.

1. A _____ is a small, new company.

2. If a company or product has a(n) _____, it has an early lead over its rivals.

3. A machine that works _____ does things automatically and on its own.

4. _____ medicine can be bought without needing approval from a doctor.

5. If something is sold _____, it is quite expensive.

PREDICTING **B.** What kind of products would be suitable for drone delivery? Note your ideas with a partner.

_____

_____

SEQUENCE   **A.** **How do you think a Flirtey drone completes a delivery? Order the steps (1–7). Then watch the video to check your ideas.**

Step _____: The drone lowers its package.

Step _____: The package is loaded onto the drone.

Step _____: The drone flies back to its headquarters.

Step __1__: A customer makes an order with a smartphone.

Step _____: The drone takes off from Flirtey's headquarters.

Step _____: The drone uses GPS to fly to the customer's location.

Step _____: The drone hovers about 15 meters in the air.

DETAILS   **B.** **Watch the video again. Are the following statements true or false, or is the information not mentioned? Circle T (true), F (false), or NG (not given).**

1.	The Flirtey delivery service is still waiting for government approval.	**T**	**F**	**NG**
2.	The company has tested several different drone models.	**T**	**F**	**NG**
3.	The drones can deliver hot food such as pizza.	**T**	**F**	**NG**
4.	The company hopes to complete local deliveries within 10 minutes.	**T**	**F**	**NG**
5.	The drones are powered by solar panels.	**T**	**F**	**NG**

CRITICAL THINKING Evaluating Pros and Cons   Work in a small group. Imagine that drone deliveries become extremely common. What might be some pros and cons of this? Consider areas such as:

practical issues   safety   long-term effects on society

_____

_____

VOCABULARY REVIEW

Do you remember the meanings of these words? Check (✓) the ones you know. Look back at the unit and review any words you're not sure of.

Reading A

☐ actual   ☐ alter*   ☐ conference*   ☐ conversely*   ☐ demonstrate*

☐ downside   ☐ get to   ☐ go over   ☐ passive*   ☐ treat

Reading B

☐ affordable   ☐ aid*   ☐ ambitious   ☐ assess*   ☐ medical

☐ military*   ☐ package   ☐ rapid   ☐ sufficient*   ☐ survey*

* Academic Word List

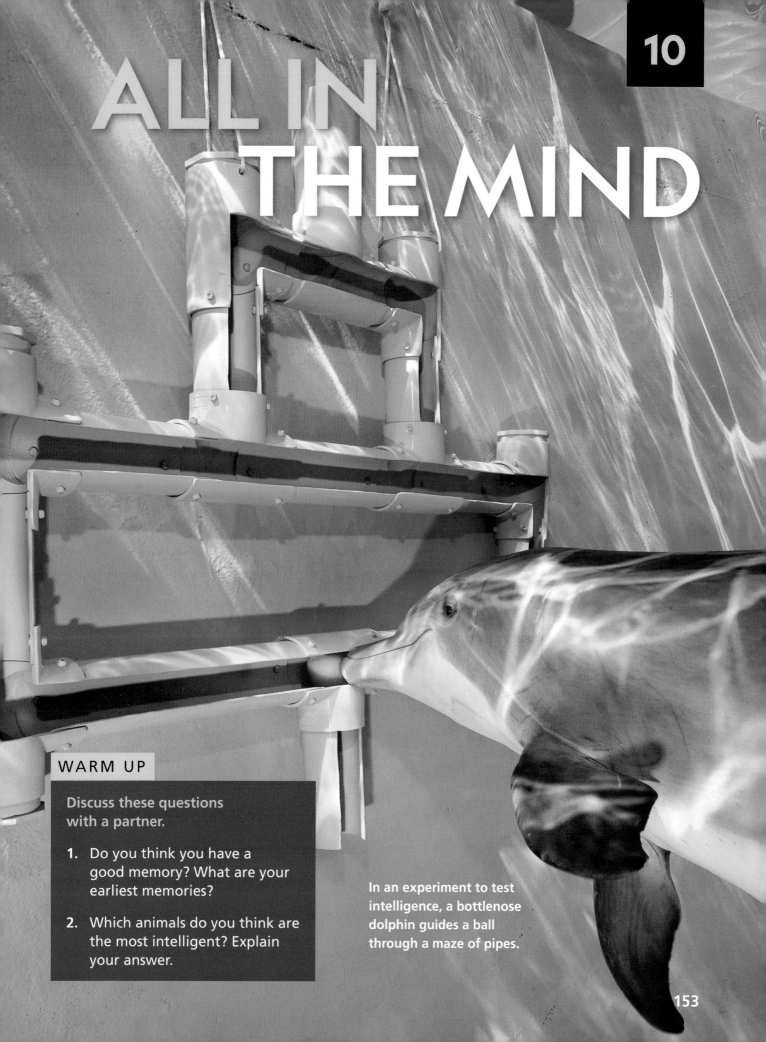

ALL IN THE MIND

WARM UP

Discuss these questions with a partner.

1. Do you think you have a good memory? What are your earliest memories?

2. Which animals do you think are the most intelligent? Explain your answer.

In an experiment to test intelligence, a bottlenose dolphin guides a ball through a maze of pipes.

10A

BEFORE YOU READ

DISCUSSION   **A.** What are some amazing things that the human brain can do? Make a list with a partner.

_____

_____

_____

PREDICTING   **B.** Which of these brain functions do you think most shape our identity? Discuss with a partner. Then read to check your ideas.

- ☐ ability to store memories
- ☐ ability to express emotions
- ☐ being aware of your own feelings

WHAT'S ON YOUR MIND?

A hearing specialist studies the brain's electrical activity as a participant performs music.

A The ancient Egyptians thought so little of the brain that when a king died, they removed the brain from his body and threw it away. The Egyptians presumed, like many people before and after them, that consciousness—your mind and your thoughts—existed in the heart.

B Now we know that the mind is a product of the brain, but how exactly does this 1.5-kilo piece of matter create a mind that allows you to think about yourself, experience happiness and anger, or remember events that happened 20 minutes or 20 years ago? This isn't a new question. Today, however, powerful new techniques for visualizing the sources of thought, **emotion**, behavior, and memory are **transforming** the way we understand the brain and the mind it creates.

C Have you ever stopped and thought, "What's wrong with me today? I just don't feel like myself"? Perhaps you were more tired or worried than usual—but somehow, you knew that something was different about you. This self-awareness—the ability to think about yourself and how you're feeling—is an important part of being human.

D This part of your mind has its origins in the prefrontal cortex—a region of your brain just behind your forehead that extends to about your ears. Before this area began to **function** (around age two), you didn't understand that you were a separate individual with your own identity. As this part of your brain developed, you became more aware of yourself and your thoughts and feelings. The temporal lobe—a part of the brain associated with perception and speech—helped you understand and put into words these thoughts and feelings.

E Perhaps one of the most important factors involved in shaping our identity is memory. What exactly is a memory? Most scientists define it as a stored pattern of connections between neurons[1] in the brain. Every feeling you remember and every thought you think alters the connections within the **vast** network of brain cells, and memories are **reinforced**, weakened, or newly formed.

---

1 A **neuron** is a cell that is part of the nervous system. Neurons send messages to and from the brain.

F Most people's earliest memories reach back to about age three or so. Very few people remember anything before this time because the part of the brain that helps form long-term memories (the hippocampus) was not yet fully developed. This doesn't mean earlier memories don't exist in your mind, though. Some scientists believe highly emotional memories, especially those associated with intense fear, might be stored in another **structure** in the brain (the amygdala) that may be functional at birth. Although these memories are not accessible to the **conscious** mind, they might still shape the way we feel and behave, even into adulthood.

G But where do our emotions come from, and how do they shape the people we are and the way we perceive the world? Forty years ago, psychologist Paul Ekman demonstrated that facial expressions used to exhibit certain emotions are recognized by people everywhere. Ekman suggested that these emotions and their corresponding facial expressions evolved to help us deal quickly with situations that can affect our **welfare**.

H Though humans may share certain emotions and recognize them in others, we don't all have the same emotional response to every situation. In fact, most emotional responses are learned and stored in our memories. The smell of freshly cut grass, for example, will generate happy feelings in someone who spent enjoyable childhood summers in the countryside, but not in someone who was forced to work long hours on a farm. Once an emotional association like this is made, it is very difficult to reverse it. "Emotion is the least **flexible** part of the brain," says Ekman. But we can learn to control our emotions by becoming consciously aware of their underlying causes and by not reacting automatically to things in our environment.

I But is it really possible to control our emotions? Researcher Richard Davidson has demonstrated that people who experience negative emotions display activity in their right prefrontal cortex. In those with a more positive **perspective**, the activity occurs in the left prefrontal cortex. Could we, Davidson wondered, control this activity and shift our mental state away from negative feelings toward a calmer state of mind?

J To answer this question, Davidson worked with a group of volunteers in the United States. One group received eight weeks of training using different meditation[2] and relaxation techniques, while another group did not. By the end of the study, those who had meditated had accomplished their goal: They showed a clear shift in brain activity toward the left, "happier" frontal cortex.

K For centuries, people have studied the brain, but it is only in recent years that we have really started to learn how it works. Nevertheless, there is still a long way to go before we understand our mind's many complexities.

---

2 **Meditation** is the act of staying silent and calm for a period of time for spiritual reasons, or to relax.

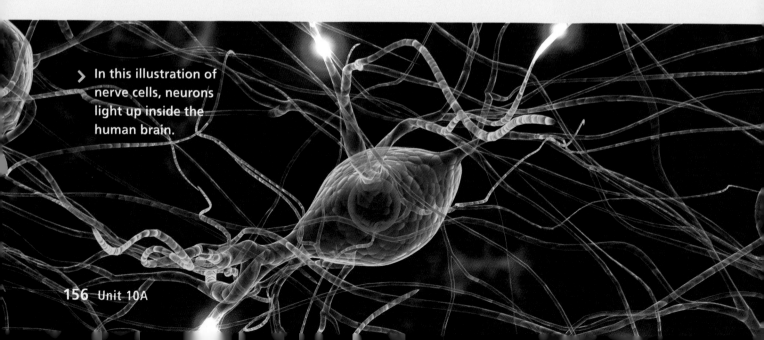

> In this illustration of nerve cells, neurons light up inside the human brain.

A. Choose the best answer for each question.

GIST   **1.** What is this reading mainly about?

    a. how we create memories   c. how the mind works

    b. mind reading   d. how emotions are processed

DETAIL   **2.** Which of these statements is NOT true?

    a. Self-awareness develops before the age of two.

    b. The prefrontal cortex affects a person's emotions.

    c. The prefrontal cortex is located at the front of the brain.

    d. New experiences change the connections between our brain cells.

DETAIL   **3.** Why don't most people have memories of what happened before they were three years old?

    a. The prefrontal cortex is not functioning well at this stage.

    b. Early memories disappear soon after they are formed.

    c. The part of the brain that forms long-term memories is not fully developed.

    d. Children tend to forget emotional memories.

DETAIL   **4.** Where is the activity center for negative emotions?

    a. in the temporal lobe   c. in the left prefrontal cortex

    b. in the hippocampus   d. in the right prefrontal cortex

DETAIL   **5.** According to researcher Richard Davidson, what helps people shift away from a negative state of mind?

    a. meditation and relaxation

    b. memory-retention techniques

    c. changing facial expressions

    d. being conscious of underlying emotions

LABELING   **B. Use information from the reading passage to match the parts of the brain with their function (1–4).**

1. helps people form long-term memories

2. stores emotional memories, such as fear

3. is associated with speech and perception

4. is key to an individual's self-awareness

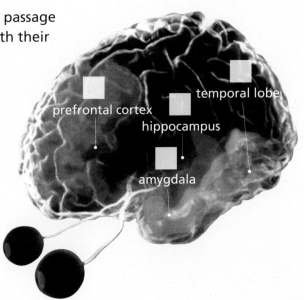

prefrontal cortex

temporal lobe

hippocampus

amygdala

Identifying Text Organization

Longer reading passages are often organized into sections, each focusing on one main idea; these sections may each consist of one paragraph or more. Some texts label sections with headings; others do not, so it is up to the reader to determine the sections and ideas. One way to quickly identify sections and main ideas is to read the first line of each paragraph and skim the rest. Understanding each section's main idea can be useful for creating a word web to summarize the reading.

IDENTIFYING MAIN IDEAS

A. Look back at the reading "What's On Your Mind?" Match the best heading (a–e) to each section. There is one extra heading.

_____ Section 1 (paragraphs C–D)   a. Who am I?

_____ Section 2 (paragraphs E–F)   b. Why do I have emotions?

_____ Section 3 (paragraphs G–H)   c. How do I remember?

_____ Section 4 (paragraphs I–J)   d. Can I control how I feel?

                                   e. Am I intelligent?

SUMMARIZING

B. Complete the summary of each section with one word or number from the reading.

Section 1

[1]_____—the ability to think about yourself—is a key part of being [2]_____. This ability begins to function at around age [3]_____.

Section 2

Memories shape our [4]_____. [5]_____ memories are formed in the hippocampus, but more intense emotional memories may be stored in the amygdala.

Our Brain and Mind

Section 3

While many emotions are universal, people have different emotional [6]_____. It can be difficult to [7]_____ emotional associations.

Section 4

In an experiment, people used [8]_____ and relaxation techniques to shift from negative to positive emotions.

CRITICAL THINKING Applying Concepts

▶ What example of an emotional association does the author mention? Underline it.

▶ Can you think of any examples from your own personal experience? Note your ideas.

_____

_____

VOCABULARY PRACTICE

COMPLETION **A.** Complete the information using words from the box. One word is extra.

conscious	perspective	reinforce	transform	vast

According to British researcher Tony Buzan, one way to improve your memory is "mind-mapping." A mind map is a diagram that shows connections between ideas. From Buzan's ¹_____, mind-mapping is a tool that can ²_____ your mental ability dramatically. One benefit is that it can help you memorize a ³_____ amount of information. Looking at a mind map again and again can also help ⁴_____ your knowledge of the information, thus allowing you to memorize it more effectively.

DEFINITIONS **B.** Complete the definitions using the words in the box.

conscious	emotions	flexible	functions	structure	welfare

1. A(n) _____ object or material can be bent easily without breaking.
2. The _____ of something is the way in which its parts are arranged.
3. If something _____ properly, it works the way it's supposed to.
4. The _____ of a person or group is their health, comfort, and happiness.
5. If you are _____, you are aware of your surroundings.
6. Joy, fear, hate, and love are examples of _____.

COLLOCATIONS **C.** The words in the box are frequently used with the adjective **vast**. Complete the sentences with the correct words. One word is extra.

areas	assortment	crowd	majority	network	number

1. There is a vast _____ of stars in our universe: billions.
2. While astronomers have mapped parts of the universe, there are vast _____ of space that they haven't.
3. The vast _____ of Americans—over 80 percent—live in urban areas.
4. The Internet is a vast _____ of interconnected computers that allows people to communicate.
5. Many people keep a vast _____ of souvenirs, letters, and photos to remind them of their past.

10B

BEFORE YOU READ

Tool use may be one indication of intelligence. Primates such as chimps and orangutans use leaves as drinking tools or for protection from rain. Even birds such as crows have shown problem-solving skills and creativity by using tools such as metal wire to obtain food.

INSIDE ANIMAL MINDS

A In 1977, Irene Pepperberg, a recent graduate of Harvard University, did something very unusual. Pepperberg was interested in learning if animals could think, and the best way to do this, she reasoned, was to talk to them. To test her **theory**, she bought an African gray parrot she named Alex and taught him to reproduce the sounds of the English language. "I thought if he learned to communicate, I could ask him questions about how he sees the world," she explains.

B When Pepperberg began her research with Alex, very few scientists **acknowledged** that animals were capable of thought. The general belief was that animals reacted to things in their environment but lacked the ability to think or feel. How, then, could a scientist demonstrate that animals might, in fact, **possess** intelligence? "That's why I started my studies with Alex," Pepperberg says.

C Certain skills are considered key signs of higher mental abilities: a good memory, an understanding of symbols,[1] self-awareness, understanding of others' **motives**, and creativity. Little by little, researchers have documented these abilities in other species. Sheep and elephants can recognize faces. Chimpanzees—who are genetically similar to humans—use a variety of **primitive** tools for eating, drinking, and hunting; they also laugh when pleased and spit[2] to show they dislike something. Octopuses in captivity[3] are known to amuse themselves by shooting water at laboratory staff. They may even exhibit basic emotions by changing color.

D Alex the parrot was a surprisingly good talker. He learned how to use his voice to **imitate** almost 100 English words, including those for foods, colors, shapes, and numbers. Although imitation was once considered a simple skill, in recent years, scientists have revealed that it's an extremely difficult ability. Because Alex had **mastered** many English words, Pepperberg could ask him questions about a bird's basic understanding of the world. Alex could count, as well as describe shapes, colors, and sizes for Pepperberg; he even had an elementary understanding of the **abstract** concept of zero.

---

1 A **symbol** is something that stands for or represents something else.
2 If you **spit**, you force liquid out of your mouth.
3 An animal in **captivity** lives in a zoo, a cage, or other enclosed place.

∧ **Kanzi, a bonobo, has learned the meaning of over 150 symbols.**

E Many of Alex's cognitive[4] skills, such as his ability to understand the concepts of "same" and "different," are generally attributed only to higher mammals, particularly primates such as humans and apes. But parrots, like great apes (and humans), live a long time in complex societies. And like primates, these birds must monitor the changing relationships within the group. This may explain Alex's ability to learn a human language. "When we take [parrots] into captivity, what they start to do is treat us as their flock,"[5] explains Pepperberg. Parrots learn to **pronounce** and use our words so they can become a part of our group.

F Researchers in Germany and Austria have also been studying language ability in dogs. One named Betsy has shown that she is able to learn and remember words as quickly as a two-year-old child. She has a vocabulary of over 340 words, knows at least 15 people by name, and can link photographs with the objects they represent. Like Alex, she's pretty smart.

---

4 Examples of **cognitive** skills include remembering, thinking, and reasoning.
5 A **flock** of birds is a group of birds.

∧ **Alex, an African gray parrot, had a large vocabulary and was able to answer questions about his understanding of the world.**

G This is the larger lesson of animal cognition research: We are not alone in our ability to invent, communicate, demonstrate emotions, or think about ourselves. Still, humans remain the creative species. No other animal has built cities, created music, or made a computer. In fact, a number of critics **dismiss** animals' ability to use tools or understand human language. They believe animals are just copying human behavior.

H Yet many researchers say that creativity and language in animals, like other forms of intelligence, have evolved. "People were surprised to discover that chimpanzees make tools," says Alex Kacelnik, an animal researcher at Oxford University. "But people also thought, 'Well, they share our ancestry—of course they're smart.' Now we're finding these kinds of behaviors in some species of birds. But we don't have a recently shared ancestry with birds . . . It means that evolution can invent similar forms of advanced intelligence more than once—that it's not something reserved only for primates or mammals."

A. Choose the best answer for each question.

GIST
1. What is this reading mainly about?
   a. ways of teaching animals to become more intelligent
   b. research that shows intelligence is not limited to humans
   c. how animals can communicate with humans
   d. how human and animal intelligence is different

DETAIL
2. Which of the following is NOT mentioned in the passage?
   a. how an octopus displays basic emotions
   b. ways in which elephants communicate with each other
   c. examples of the tool-making abilities of chimpanzees
   d. the language abilities of a dog

DETAIL
3. What could Alex do that especially helped Irene Pepperberg to conduct her research?
   a. count
   b. describe colors
   c. copy human language
   d. understand the concept of zero

VOCABULARY
4. In paragraph F, the word *link* could be replaced with _____.
   a. match   c. count
   b. take   d. view

DETAIL
5. What do parrots and primates have in common?
   a. They both live a long time in complex societies.
   b. They both learn to use tools while in captivity.
   c. They both teach new human words to their young.
   d. Neither likes to participate in or be part of a group.

INFERRING
INFORMATION

B. Can you infer the statements below from the information given in the passage? Circle Yes or No.

Review This Skill in Unit 8B

1. Irene Pepperberg had tested her theory before buying Alex. (paragraph B) **Yes   No**

2. Chimpanzees have some of the same emotional reactions as humans do. (paragraph C) **Yes   No**

3. Alex accepted Pepperberg as part of his flock. (paragraph E) **Yes   No**

4. Betsy the dog learned words in the same order as a two-year-old. (paragraph F) **Yes   No**

5. Parrots such as Alex can think creatively. (paragraph H) **Yes   No**

Recognizing Lexical Cohesion (1)

Lexical cohesion is a feature of good writing. Writers often use different words to avoid repetition and to add variety to a text. One way to achieve this is to use synonyms. Sometimes, instead of two words being exact synonyms, one word may be a more specific (or a more general) part of, or an example of, another word. Look at the following examples.

The aroma in the kitchen got my attention. The smell of cookies took me back to my childhood.
(Here, *aroma* and *smell* refer to the same thing.)

I bought flour, sugar, and cocoa. After I got the ingredients home, I realized I had no vanilla.
(Here, flour, sugar, cocoa, and vanilla are specific examples of ingredients.)

RECOGNIZING SYNONYMS **A.** These words are from the reading passage. Find pairs of synonyms and write them below.

actions	basic	behaviors	communicate	create
elementary	exhibit	invent	show	talk

1. _____ = _____
2. _____ = _____
3. _____ = _____
4. _____ = _____
5. _____ = _____

ANALYZING **B.** In each extract below, circle the general term and underline any specific examples of the word.

1. . . . researchers have documented these abilities in other species. Sheep and elephants can recognize faces. (paragraph C)

2. . . . particularly primates such as humans and apes. (paragraph E)

3. . . . humans remain the creative species. (paragraph G)

4. . . . researchers say that creativity and language in animals, like other forms of intelligence, have evolved. (paragraph H)

CRITICAL THINKING Evaluating Using Criteria

▸ According to the reading, what are the five skills that show an animal has intelligence? Underline them.

▸ How would you rate Alex the parrot's intelligence based on the five skills? Share your ideas with a partner.

COMPLETION   **A.** Complete the paragraph using words from the box. One word is extra.

abstract	acknowledges	dismiss	mastered	primitive

Research in Senegal has shown that chimpanzees seem to have
¹_____ the art of basic tool-making. Furthermore, a chimp
was observed sharpening a stick with her teeth before using it as a(n)
²_____ tool for killing a bush baby.[1]

Some researchers ³_____ the significance of these findings.
Primatologist Craig Stanford, for example, ⁴_____ that the
behavior is fascinating but suggests that the research might simply be
". . . a short note in a journal." However, researcher Jill Pruetz claims
that the discovery shows that chimp behavior can be very humanlike.

_____

1 A **bush baby** is a small animal with large eyes that lives in Africa.

∧ Chimps have been observed using tools for drinking.

DEFINITIONS   **B.** Complete the sentences with words from the box.

abstract	imitate	motive	possess	pronounce	theory

1. To _____ something means to have or own it.
2. If you _____ someone, you copy what they do.
3. To _____ a word means to say it using particular sounds.
4. Your _____ for doing something is your reason for doing it.
5. If something is _____, it's an idea rather than an actual object.
6. A _____ is an idea that scientists test to see if it's true.

WORD LINK   **C.** The word **pronounce** includes the root *nounce* which means "say" or "call." Complete the sentences with words from the box. One word is extra.

announced	denounce	pronounce	renounce

1. In June 2018, FIFA _____ that the co-hosts of the 2026 soccer World Cup will be Canada, Mexico, and the United States.
2. All political leaders must _____ the use of violence by their supporters.
3. British place names such as Norwich, Edinburgh, and Leicester can be hard to _____ correctly.

BRAIN
POWER

BEFORE YOU WATCH

DEFINITIONS **A.** Read the information. The words and phrases in **bold** appear in the video. Match the words and phrases to their definitions.

The brain **is made up** of millions of neurons (or nerve cells) and nerve fibers connected to our nervous system. This system allows the brain to **regulate** basic body functions, like respiration (breathing), and **coordinate** the flow of information. **Sensory** information travels to the brain via the nervous system. Motor **signals**—information that tells our body what to do—travel out from our brain within a few microseconds.

1. is made up (of) •   • related to touch, sight, hearing, etc.

2. regulate •   • consists of

3. sensory •   • to control the speed or performance of something

4. signal •   • an action that sends a message

5. coordinate •   • to bring different parts together so they work well

PREVIEW **B.** What other body functions, apart from breathing, does the brain regulate? Make a list with a partner.

_____

_____

_____

MAIN IDEAS **A.** Watch the video. Match the functions (a–d) to the parts of the brain.

a. Controls weight regulation, and behaviors like eating and drinking.

b. Controls muscle movements and the body's balance.

c. Controls heart activity, respiration, digestion, and sleep.

d. Controls learning, reasoning, speech, and the senses.

CEREBRUM DIENCEPHALON

BRAIN STEM CEREBELLUM

TRUE OR FALSE **B.** Watch the video again. Circle if the following statements are true (T) or false (F).

1. The cerebrum takes up about half of the brain's volume.   **T   F**

2. Nerve fibers carry signals to the spinal cord.   **T   F**

3. The brain stem is made of four parts.   **T   F**

4. Chemicals are produced in the brain's core.   **T   F**

CRITICAL THINKING Synthesizing Ideas   Consider what you have learned in this unit about cognition research. In what ways do you think the findings might be important? How might they help people in the future? Discuss your ideas with a partner.

_____

_____

VOCABULARY REVIEW

Do you remember the meanings of these words? Check (✓) the ones you know. Look back at the unit and review any words you're not sure of.

Reading A

☐ conscious   ☐ emotion   ☐ flexible*   ☐ function*   ☐ perspective*

☐ reinforce*   ☐ structure*   ☐ transform*   ☐ vast   ☐ welfare*

Reading B

☐ abstract   ☐ acknowledge*   ☐ dismiss   ☐ imitate   ☐ master

☐ motive*   ☐ possess   ☐ primitive   ☐ pronounce   ☐ theory*

* Academic Word List

11

VISUAL PIONEERS

A visitor admires an oil painting by Joan Miró in the National Museum of Western Art, Tokyo, Japan.

Discuss these questions with a partner.

1. Who are some of the greatest artists of all time? What makes these artists great?

2. Besides paintings, how else can people represent the world visually?

169

A self-portrait by the artist Vincent van Gogh on display in Amsterdam, the Netherlands

BEFORE YOU READ

QUIZ **A.** How much do you know about the artist Vincent van Gogh? Circle your answers.

1. Van Gogh was *Belgian / French / Dutch.*

2. He was born in *1823 / 1853 / 1903.*

3. He decided to be a painter at age *6 / 16 / 26.*

4. He is famous for painting *red roses / yellow sunflowers / white lilies.*

SCANNING **B.** Scan the first two paragraphs on the next page to check your answers. Then read the rest of the passage.

VAN GOGH'S WORLD

A Starry nights and sunflowers, self-portraits and café settings—all painted in bold, intense colors. Today, people around the world immediately recognize these as the work of Vincent van Gogh, the Dutch painter. Probably no other artist, at any time in any culture, has achieved such popularity. But who was this man and why, even today, do his art and life have such an ability to move us?

An Artist Is Born

B Vincent van Gogh was born on March 30, 1853, in Zundert, a small village in southern Holland. As a child, he was serious and **sensitive**. He loved to draw, and his work showed talent, but no one encouraged him to become an artist. Instead, his father thought he should take a "**sensible**" job—something like a salesclerk or carpenter. As a young adult, he **wandered** from job to job with little success and very little money, becoming more depressed with each failure. In March 1880, however, just before his 27th birthday, something changed inside van Gogh. He realized that he was meant to be a painter, and he began to study art in Brussels, receiving financial help from his brother Theo.

Discovering Color

C In 1886, van Gogh moved to Paris, hoping to learn more about the color techniques being used by Impressionist artists there. Instead of grays and browns, his work began to emphasize blue and red, and then yellow and orange. Soon he began to see life differently: *Go slow. Stop thinking. Look around. You'll see something beautiful if you open yourself.* These were the principles that guided his art. With his **innovative** color combinations, van Gogh wanted to show others how to better **appreciate** a flower, the night sky, or a person's face.

Descent into Madness

D Few who lived in van Gogh's time appreciated his work, however. Many laughed when they saw his paintings, which hurt the sensitive artist terribly. In February 1888, he moved away from Paris to Arles, a town in southern France. Often he could not eat or sleep, and stayed up into the early morning hours painting. Days passed, and he spoke to no one. Following an argument with fellow artist Paul Gauguin, van Gogh took a razor and cut off his own earlobe.[1]

---

1 Your **earlobe** is the soft part at the bottom of your ear.

▲ *The Starry Night*, **painted in June 1889**

E He never explained why he injured himself, but by now, many were convinced that van Gogh was crazy, and, indeed, his mental health started to decline. He began to have attacks during which he would hear strange sounds and think people were trying to hurt him. In the spring of 1889, he was sent to a mental hospital in Saint-Rémy, a town near Arles.

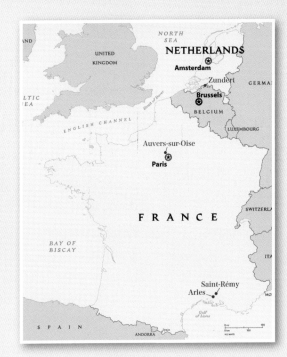

F What exactly was van Gogh suffering from? No one knows for certain, but some now think it may have been a form of manic depression.[2] Whatever his condition, van Gogh's illness both inhibited and inspired his **creativity**. When his attacks came, he could not paint. But during his periods of calm, he was able to complete more than a hundred masterpieces, including the **classic** *The Starry Night*. "Working on my pictures," he wrote, "is almost a necessity for my **recovery**."

G Following his release from the hospital in May 1890, van Gogh took a room in Auvers-sur-Oise, a town just north of Paris. For the 70 days that he lived there, he produced, on average, a painting a day. Until his death, however, he was unable to sell a single one; today, those paintings would be worth more than a billion U.S. dollars.

H It was at this time that van Gogh either borrowed or stole a gun. On the afternoon of July 27, 1890, he went out to the country and shot himself in the stomach. Two days later, Vincent van Gogh died at age 37. What caused him to take his own life—his lack of financial success, mental illness, loneliness?

Van Gogh's Legacy[3]

I Over a century after his death, van Gogh remains extremely popular. His story—of a man who **resisted** materialism[4] and greed, who was alone and unappreciated—gives people something they need. We find pieces of ourselves in him. This may also explain the high prices paid for van Gogh's work. His *Portrait of Dr. Gachet* sold in 1990 for more than $80 million to a Japanese businessman, breaking the world record for a painting. Many of his other works have also sold for millions. Of course, people are buying great art when they **purchase** one of van Gogh's paintings, but they are also buying a piece of his story, which, like his work, will live on forever.

---

2 **Manic depression** is a medical condition in which one feels alternately excited and depressed.

3 A **legacy** is something that comes from someone in the past.

4 **Materialism** is attaching a lot of importance to money and having a lot of things.

A. Choose the best answer for each question.

DETAIL

1. Which statement is NOT true about van Gogh's youth?

   a. He grew up in Holland.

   b. He was born in a small village.

   c. His parents encouraged his artistic talent.

   d. He tried several jobs, but was unsuccessful.

PURPOSE

2. What is the purpose of paragraph B?

   a. to give information about van Gogh's birthplace

   b. to describe how van Gogh became a painter

   c. to show that van Gogh was a troubled man

   d. to explain how van Gogh survived on his own

^ **A café in Arles made famous by van Gogh's** *Café Terrace at Night*

MAIN IDEA

3. What is the main idea in paragraph C?

   a. Van Gogh was unhappy working with painters in Holland.

   b. Van Gogh's move to Paris changed his attitude toward art.

   c. Van Gogh was less successful than other Impressionist painters.

   d. Van Gogh's paintings of flowers were very popular in Paris.

PARAPHRASE

4. Which of the following is closest in meaning to *Working on my pictures is almost a necessity for my recovery.* (paragraph F)?

   a. I need to paint in order to heal myself.

   b. I need to get better so that I can paint again.

   c. I will improve only if I stop painting.

   d. I will paint only after I feel better.

COHESION

5. The following sentence would best be placed at the end of which paragraph?
The question, like so many others in van Gogh's life, remains unanswered.

   a. Paragraph E   b. Paragraph F   c. Paragraph G   d. Paragraph H

SEQUENCING

B. Number the events in van Gogh's life in the order they occurred (1–6). Then sketch the route he took during his life on the map on the previous page.

_____ showed artistic talent in his hometown, Zundert

_____ argued with artist Paul Gauguin in Arles

_____ produced a painting a day for over two months in Auvers

_____ studied the techniques of Impressionist painters in Paris

_____ moved to Brussels to learn the skills needed to be an artist

_____ sent to a mental hospital in Saint-Rémy

Inferring Information (2)

As a reader, it may be possible to infer information that is not stated directly in a text. Sometimes we can use information and arguments in the text to infer things that are *probably* true. When you infer something, think about what evidence or information led you to make the inference.

INFERRING   **A.** Are the statements (1–7) probably true based on information in the passage? Check (✓) five statements that we can infer, and underline the part(s) of the text that support each inference.

☐ **1.** Van Gogh's father likely disagreed with his son's choice to become a painter.

☐ **2.** Theo, van Gogh's brother, probably supported Vincent's artistic ambitions.

☐ **3.** In Arles, van Gogh probably had several close friends.

☐ **4.** The argument with Gauguin may have led to van Gogh cutting his own ear.

☐ **5.** The doctors in Saint-Rémy likely did not cure van Gogh's illness.

☐ **6.** Van Gogh probably completed some of his best work while in the hospital.

☐ **7.** Van Gogh seems to have given up painting in the last two months of his life.

INFERRING   **B.** Note answers to each question by inferring information from the passage. Then discuss your ideas with a partner.

1. What factors may have led van Gogh to becoming a painter?

_____

2. What is a likely reason van Gogh decided to leave Paris?

_____

3. What might have led to van Gogh's self-injury?

_____

CRITICAL THINKING Evaluating Evidence

▶ The author suggests three factors may have contributed to van Gogh taking his own life. List the evidence, if any, that the author provides for each one.

Lack of financial success	Mental illness	Loneliness

▶ Which do you think was probably the most important factor? Discuss your ideas with a partner.

COMPLETION   **A.** Complete the information with the correct form of words from the box.

appreciate	classic	innovative	resist	wander

Many Impressionist painters greatly admired Japanese woodblock prints—images created by stamping inked wooden images onto paper. These techniques were new and ¹_____ to Europeans. Van Gogh ²_____ the work of Japanese woodblock artists, such as Hiroshige. During the time van Gogh spent ³_____ the fields near Arles, he felt a close relationship with Japanese art and culture, and even shaved his head to look like a Japanese monk. However, many other Western artists ⁴_____ this new movement and argued instead for the use of older, ⁵_____ painting techniques.

⌃ **In 1887, van Gogh created** ***Bridge in the Rain,*** **a version of this woodcut by Hiroshige.**

DEFINITIONS   **B.** Complete the sentences. Choose the correct options.

   1. If someone shows **creativity**, they have many *original / traditional* ideas.

   2. When you **recover** from an illness or injury, you become *well again / sicker*.

   3. If a decision is **sensible**, it usually means it is based on *emotion / reason*.

   4. If you are **sensitive** to other people's feelings, you are *aware / not aware* of them.

   5. If you **purchase** something, you *buy / sell* it.

   6. If a work of art is **classic**, it's considered to be of *poor / great* quality.

WORD LINK   **C.** The word root **sen(s)**, as in **sensible**, means "feeling or being aware." Complete the sentences with the correct words from the box.

sensation	senseless	sensible	sensitive

   1. Getting a new job before you quit your old one is the _____ thing to do.

   2. As I entered the house, I had a strange _____ that I'd been there before.

   3. The museum was shocked by the _____ act of violence against the painting.

   4. Good teachers should always be _____ to the needs of their students.

BEFORE YOU READ

DISCUSSION **A.** How would you describe the painting below and those on the next two pages? Use the words below or your own ideas. Use a dictionary to help you. Share your ideas with a partner.

abstract	**colorful**	**personal**	**playful**
political	**realistic**	**surreal**	**vivid**

PREDICTING **B.** You are going to read about an influential artist and a mysterious photographer. Look at the images, and read the captions and titles. Why do you think the work of each artist is important? Read the passage to check your answers.

△ *Operarios* (1933) by the painter Tarsila do Amaral shows a diverse group of workers in an industrial city setting.

SEEING THE LIGHT

In recent years, the artistic achievements of two 20th-century pioneers have been brought to a global audience.

< In 1995, Tarsila's *Abaporu* was sold at auction for $1.4 million, making it the most valuable painting ever by a Brazilian artist.

THE PICASSO OF BRAZIL

A   In 2018, a major new exhibition opened at New York's Museum of Modern Art (MoMA). The show brought together more than a hundred works by a single Brazilian artist: Tarsila do Amaral. Although widely celebrated in her **native** country, the artist was relatively unknown outside Brazil. So who was Tarsila?

B   Born in 1886 in a small town near São Paulo, Tarsila do Amaral is considered the mother of modern art in Brazil. She first developed a love for art after her parents sent her to study in Spain. She returned to Europe a few years later, and **settled** in Paris. Several artists there, including Picasso, were beginning to experiment with new forms—less realistic and more abstract. The new approaches continued to **influence** Tarsila after she returned to Brazil.

C   Approaches to art in Brazil at that time were relatively **conservative**. Traditional European **styles** dominated, with works mainly featuring natural, religious, or historical scenes in soft colors. Tarsila decided to take a different direction: "I want to be the painter of my country," she wrote. Her images began to **reflect** Brazil's diverse identity—a mix of native, African, and European peoples. She used strong, vivid colors to paint real-life scenes of the nation's farmers, countryside, and wildlife. This had never been done before in Brazilian art.

∧ *A Cuca* (1924). "I want to be the painter of my country," Tarsila wrote.

D One of Tarsila's most famous works is *Abaporu* (1928). The title combines two words from Tupi-Guarani[1] languages, meaning "Man Who Eats People." The painting has a playful, surreal[2] quality—but its look and feel are distinctly Brazilian. The work—and its title—later inspired a Brazilian art movement called *antropofagia*, or cannibalism.[3] Brazilian artists began to take in—or "digest"— styles from other cultures and mix them with local influences. The result was something uniquely Brazilian.

E Tarsila do Amaral died in São Paulo in 1973, age 86, after a career spanning six decades. But her artwork and legacy live on in her native Brazil. "For Brazilians, her recognition is kind of off the charts," says James Rondeau, director of the Art Institute of Chicago. "She is the Picasso of Brazil." Now, with the MoMA exhibition and other international shows, Tarsila's art is being appreciated by a new audience of admirers around the world.

---

1 **Tupi-Guarani** is a group of native American languages spoken in parts of South America.

2 A **surreal** art style shows objects or a scene in a strange or dreamlike way.

3 In a cultural context, **cannibalism** is the taking of an idea from one place or context and using it in another.

THE SECRET PHOTOGRAPHER

F At first, they seemed like ordinary photographs. A couple holding hands. A child standing by a dirty window. A man daydreaming in a park. The images were hidden in boxes for years, unseen except by the woman who took them: Vivian Maier. But when a collector bought some of the boxes at auction, he soon realized their contents were remarkable. Maier's street scenes might seem ordinary, but they were actually very special.

G Vivian Maier was born in New York City in 1926, the daughter of French and Austrian **immigrants**. For most of her early life, she moved between New York and Europe. In 1956, she moved to Chicago, where she worked as a nanny[4] and caregiver. In her free time, she walked the city streets, taking pictures and developing her photography skills. It was a hobby she would continue for the rest of her life.

H Maier's black-and-white images mostly portray **urban** life: street scenes and regular people. Residents carry out everyday tasks—shopping, riding on buses, walking in a park. Often, she took her pictures in secret. People are caught acting naturally, unaware that they are being photographed. Many of the photos reveal something personal—and often deeply moving. They show us the beauty, humor, pain, and the mystery of normal life.

▲ **A negative image reflects viewers at a Vivien Maier exhibition.**

I   In total, Maier took over 100,000 photographs, but she developed very few. Instead, she kept most of the negatives[5] and a few prints in boxes in a rented **storage** space in Chicago. Toward the end of her life, she was unable to pay rent to the storage company. So the boxes—with her work inside—were sold at auction.

J   In 2007, John Maloof purchased the contents of one of the storage lockers. Realizing the quality of the images, he added a **selection** of Maier's photographs to an image-sharing website. Thousands of people worldwide viewed the photos, and many went viral. Maier's photos began to appear in books and exhibitions. In 2015, a movie about her life—*Finding Vivian Maier*—was nominated for an Academy Award.

K   It is not known why Maier kept her photos secret, or how she might feel about her worldwide fame. She died in April 2009, in a nursing home in the Chicago suburbs. Much of Maier's life remains a mystery. But her talent as a visual storyteller—for so long hidden in darkness—has finally seen the light of day.

∧ A street scene by Vivien Maier, on display at a Los Angeles gallery

4 A **nanny** looks after children in their home while their parents are working.
5 In film photography, **negatives** are the images used to make print photos.

A Twin Lens Reflex Camera, as used by Vivian Maier

A. Choose the best answer for each question.

MAIN IDEA

1. According to the passage, both Tarsila do Amaral and Vivian Maier _____.

a. are more famous overseas than in their home country
b. were inspired by everyday scenes in their home country
c. established a major artistic movement in their home country
d. are largely unknown in their home country

DETAIL

2. Which of the following is NOT true about Tarsila do Amaral?

a. She made more than one study trip to Europe.
b. Her art was the focus of a major 2018 exhibition.
c. Her European experiences influenced her art style.
d. She painted her natural scenes using mostly soft colors.

INFERENCE

3. Which of the following would most likely be an example of *antropofagia*?

a. a drawing made by a tribesman in a remote Amazon village
b. art made by a Brazilian painter that shows European influences
c. a series of photographs taken by a European on vacation in Rio
d. an ancient cave painting discovered in the Brazilian rain forest

VOCABULARY

4. Which word or phrase is closest in meaning to *off the charts* (paragraph E)?

a. very unreliable
b. relatively unknown
c. far beyond normal
d. hard to understand

DETAIL

5. How did Vivian Maier first become internationally famous?

a. after a collector shared her photos online
b. when she starred in a major Hollywood movie
c. when she attended a major art show in New York
d. after her photos were published in a Chicago newspaper

MAIN IDEAS

B. Choose the best heading for each paragraph of "The Secret Photographer" (F–K). Two headings are extra.

1. Paragraph F _____
2. Paragraph G _____
3. Paragraph H _____
4. Paragraph I _____
5. Paragraph J _____
6. Paragraph K _____

a. New Photographic Technology
b. An End—And a New Beginning
c. A Collector Makes a Discovery
d. Beginnings of a Life in Photography
e. Disagreement Over the Images' Quality
f. Maier's Images Gain Global Appreciation
g. Capturing the Elements of Daily Life
h. Packed Away in Storage

Recognizing Lexical Cohesion (2)

In Unit 10B, you saw how writers often use synonyms as a way to avoid repetition and to make their ideas more interesting. A writer may use an exact synonym (e.g., *a great* **photo** and *a great* **shot**). Often, though, a writer will use a word or phrase that has a similar, but not an exact, meaning.

The photographer Ansel Adams was famous for his photographs of **national parks**.

His shots of **unspoiled wilderness** *continue to impress viewers today.*

Noticing the connection between related key words and phrases can help you follow an author's ideas.

IDENTIFYING SYNONYMS

A. Find synonyms in the reading for each of the underlined words.

1. Tarsila do Amaral is famous for her underlined paintings.

   paragraph A: _____   paragraph E: _____

2. She is underlined admired as a great artist.

   paragraph A: _____   paragraph E: _____

3. Her paintings are underlined clearly Brazilian.

   paragraph D: _____   paragraph D: _____

IDENTIFYING SYNONYMS

B. Answer the questions below about the reading passage.

1. In paragraph F, the author writes that Vivian Maier's scenes seemed *ordinary*. What three synonyms does the author use for this in paragraph H?

   _____

2. In paragraph F, the author describes the images as *very special*. What other synonym does the author use in that paragraph? _____

3. What synonym does the author use for *the photos reveal* later in paragraph H?

   _____

4. In paragraph K, what phrase does the author use as a synonym for the photos being *kept in secret*? _____

CRITICAL THINKING Evaluating Pros and Cons   Read paragraph K again and discuss the following questions with a partner.

▶ Why do you think artists may keep their work hidden from the public?

▶ What are the pros and cons of making an artist famous after they die? Consider the pros and cons for the following people and places:

   the artist   the artist's family   the artist's hometown/country

   the subjects the artist painted or took photos of

COMPLETION **A.** Complete the information using the correct form of the words from the box.

> | immigrant | reflect | selection | settle | urban |

Artist Nari Ward creates works of art using discarded objects from the ¹_____ neighborhoods of New York City. He repurposes used bottles, broken TVs, and abandoned shopping carts, among other objects. One of his most famous works, "We the People" was created entirely from a ²_____ of hand-dyed shoelaces.

∧ **Nari Ward with his artwork "Divination X"**

Born in Jamaica, Ward's family ³_____ in New York City in the 1970s. As an artist, his work ⁴_____ issues such as poverty, race, and consumer culture. He is the winner of the 2017 Vilcek Prize for the Arts, given annually to ⁵_____ artists who have made a significant contribution to U.S. society.

DEFINITIONS **B.** Complete the sentences. Choose the correct option.

1. An example of a photographer's **style** might be _____.
   a. the price of their latest work
   b. how they use space and light

2. If someone **influences** you, you are _____ likely to do what they do or say.
   a. less
   b. more

3. When someone dresses in a **conservative** way, they dress in a _____ way.
   a. conventional or traditional
   b. liberal or exaggerated

4. Something that you might put in **storage** is _____.
   a. a box of books
   b. a glass of water

5. If you are a **native** of a place, you are _____.
   a. from there
   b. from somewhere else

WORD LINK **C.** The word root **nat-**, as in **native**, means "birth" or "born." Choose the correct word to complete each sentence.

1. According to researchers, babies have a(n) *innate / nation* ability to learn language.

2. South America consists of 12 *nationals / nations*—the largest being Brazil.

3. Kangaroos and koalas are *innate / native* to Australia.

4. Many artists paint the *natural / native* world—such as mountains.

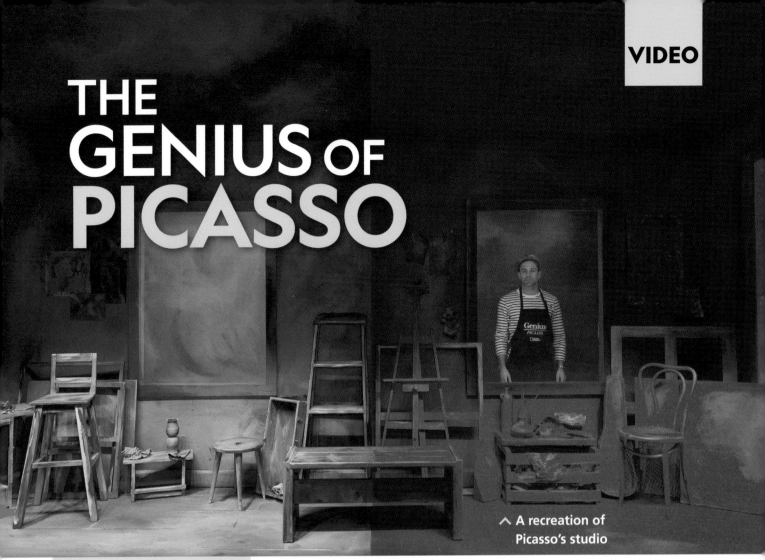

THE GENIUS OF PICASSO

∧ **A recreation of Picasso's studio**

BEFORE YOU WATCH

DEFINITIONS **A.** Read the information. The words and phrases in **bold** appear in the video. Match the words with their definitions.

Pablo Picasso (1881–1973) was one of the greatest artists of the 20th century—in fact, many think he was a **genius**. At 16, he was enrolled in the finest art school in Madrid. However, Picasso wanted to try new ideas—to **push the boundaries** of what was possible in art. Within a decade, he was producing portraits that left some viewers confused. They couldn't figure out what they were looking at: *Is this a face? Is that an arm?* Picasso would continue to **buck** traditions and **reinvent** the field of art during his long career.

1. genius   •   • to go beyond the limits

2. push the boundaries •   • to change something so that it appears to be new

3. reinvent   •   • someone with exceptional ability

4. buck   •   • to resist or oppose

PREDICTING **B.** Some scientists argue that Picasso—like other geniuses—had a "rage to master." What do you think this means? Check (✓) the best option and discuss with a partner.

☐ a strong drive or passion to succeed   ☐ an urge to teach others how to paint

☐ a need to paint differently from other people   ☐ a desire to control his anger

VIEWING **A.** Watch the video. Check your answers to the Before You Watch section.

MULTIPLE CHOICE **B.** Watch the video again. Then choose the best answer for each question.

1. According to the video, why was Picasso so creative in Paris?

a. He was around other creative people.

b. He was inspired by his family members.

2. What do you think Picasso meant by "A picture used to be a sum of additions. With me, a picture is a sum of destructions"?

a. His approach to painting is the opposite of the traditional approach.

b. His approach to painting is simpler than the traditional approach.

3. What do you think Picasso meant by "The picture lives only through the man who is looking at it"?

a. A painting only has meaning when it pushes the boundaries.

b. A painting's meaning depends on the person viewing it.

CRITICAL THINKING Synthesizing   Discuss these questions with a partner.

▶ Which of the artists featured in this unit do you think was the most talented? Why?

▶ Can you think of any people who are not appreciated as "great artists" now, but might be in the future? Note down your ideas.

VOCABULARY REVIEW

Do you remember the meanings of these words? Check (✓) the ones you know. Look back at the unit and review any words you're not sure of.

Reading A

☐ appreciate*   ☐ creativity*   ☐ purchase*   ☐ resist   ☐ sensitive

☐ classic*   ☐ innovative*   ☐ recovery*   ☐ sensible   ☐ wander

Reading B

☐ conservative   ☐ influence   ☐ reflect   ☐ settle   ☐ style

☐ immigrant*   ☐ native   ☐ selection*   ☐ storage   ☐ urban

* Academic Word List

FAR OUT

12

Astronaut Terry Virts photographs the Earth through the windows of the International Space Station.

WARM UP

Discuss these questions with a partner.

1. What are some reasons humans explore space?

2. What has been humankind's greatest achievement in space exploration?

BEFORE YOU READ

DISCUSSION

A. Read the photo caption and answer the questions.

1. What do you think this station is used for?

2. What do you think is the best part of working at the ISS? What do you think are the biggest challenges?

SKIMMING AND PREDICTING

B. Quickly skim the reading on the next two pages. What topics do you expect to learn about? Check (✓) your answers. Then read the passage to check your ideas.

☐ some common problems at the ISS

☐ possible dangers of spacewalking

☐ how a person becomes an astronaut

☐ how astronauts prepare for a spacewalk

☐ one astronaut's experience in space

> Astronauts working outside the International Space Station (ISS), a permanent space laboratory about 400 kilometers above Earth

DEFYING GRAVITY

A Italian astronaut Luca Parmitano had a terrifying experience during a spacewalk. While working on the International Space Station (ISS), his helmet[1] began filling with water.

B At first, Parmitano wasn't sure what it was. "My head is really wet," he told NASA flight controllers back on Earth. As the water began to **accumulate**, Parmitano realized there was a problem. "It's too much . . . Now it's in my eyes," he recalls saying. **Concerned** that he might choke[2] on the water, ground control stopped the spacewalk. Back inside the ISS, Parmitano took off his helmet and discovered that it contained almost half a liter of water. Where had this water come from?

C NASA found out that a malfunction[3] in the suit's liquid cooling system had caused water to leak. Some of the water got into Parmitano's helmet. Though NASA has taken steps to correct the problem, the experience underscores the dangers that astronauts face each time they **venture** outside a spacecraft.

Training for a Spacewalk

D Spacewalks are safer now than they were over 50 years ago, when—in 1965—Russian Alexei Leonov carried out the first one. However, as Parmitano's experience illustrates, there are still risks involved. To ensure that missions are successful, astronauts train on Earth for hundreds of hours. They learn to deal with the lack of gravity in space, for example, by floating in a large tank[4] of water, where they experience a feeling very close to the weightlessness of space. For every hour they will walk in space, astronauts practice for 10 hours in the water. They also **familiarize** themselves with the exact route they will take once they leave a spacecraft. They go over this path repeatedly, so they know exactly what to do on a spacewalk.

E Astronauts also train for emergencies that may come about during a walk. One of the most common is losing **consciousness**. Although spacesuits have an **internal** heating and cooling system, they can still get very hot, especially when astronauts are doing physically **demanding** work outside the spacecraft for hours. Astronauts are trained to monitor their breathing and to make sure their bodies aren't overheating, which could cause them to pass out. Another potential challenge that astronauts are trained to deal with is being separated from a spacecraft. During a walk, astronauts work in pairs and are attached to the ISS for safety reasons. Every NASA spacesuit has a mini jetpack, and astronauts are trained to use it to float back to the station if they somehow become **detached** from the craft.

---

1 A **helmet** is a protective hat made of strong material that often covers the face.
2 If you **choke** on something, you cannot breathe because something is stuck in your throat.
3 A **malfunction** is a failure to work normally.
4 A **tank** is a large container that holds liquid (like water) or gas.

SUNITA WILLIAMS: SPACEWALKER

Sunita Williams

F As a child, Sunita Williams believed that space travel would be routine when she grew up—something everyone did. She never thought she'd be one of the **pioneers**. The former pilot has now visited the International Space Station several times, and has spent dozens of hours walking in space.

National Geographic: What's the most **impressive** thing about a spacewalk?

Sunita Williams: The view—being up very high looking down and seeing the northern lights below.

NG: Is it scary?

SW: On my first walk in 2006, there was a problem with a solar array (a solar panel) on the station, and we needed to fix it. A long arm connects the space station to the array. As I started going up this arm to the array, I felt like I was climbing a skyscraper. I had to tell myself, "It's okay. You're not going to fall." In space, you can get really confused sometimes. You don't know if you are going up or down, left or right. During that first walk outside the ISS, I had to remind myself how we trained in the water tank. That helped me stay calm.

NG: Are there things you do to keep yourself grounded[5] while living in space?

SW: On my first flight, I would go down to the Russian end of the space station because there was only one bathroom at the time. Astronaut Misha Tyurin would always say, "Would you like some tea?" We would sit or float in the air for five or ten minutes drinking tea and just talk about life.

---

5 If you are **grounded**, you behave in a calm, sensible way, like a normal person.

NASA astronauts experience weightless training at the Johnson Space Center in Houston, Texas, USA.

A. Choose the best answer for each question.

CAUSE AND EFFECT

1. What caused Luca Parmitano's helmet to fill with water?

a. There was a crack in his helmet, which caused a leak.
b. A bag with drinking water inside his suit began to leak.
c. No one knows why it filled with water.
d. There was a problem with his suit's liquid cooling system.

DETAIL

2. Who was the first person to go on a spacewalk?

a. Luca Parmitano
b. Sunita Williams
c. Alexei Leonov
d. Misha Tyurin

DETAIL

3. How long does an astronaut need to practice in the water to prepare for a two-hour spacewalk?

a. 10 hours
b. 30 hours
c. 20 hours
d. hundreds of hours

REFERENCE

4. What does *it* refer to in the last sentence of paragraph E?

a. the walk
b. the jetpack
c. the spacecraft
d. the spacesuit

INFERENCE

5. What would Sunita Williams say was the most challenging aspect of her first spacewalk?

a. the fear of falling from the solar array
b. the poor visibility through her helmet
c. the confusion caused by the northern lights
d. the difficulty of fixing the solar panels

∧ **An astronaut's spacesuit provides oxygen and protects against solar rays.**

SCANNING

B. Complete the chart with words from the reading. Use one word for each item (1–6).

Challenges of a spacewalk	Training activities to help
Coping without gravity	Astronauts practice ¹_____ in water on Earth. This gives them a similar feeling of ²_____ that they will have in space.
Moving in space	Astronauts practice the ³_____ on Earth many times.
Overheating in spacesuit	Astronauts are taught to ⁴_____ their breathing and check they don't ⁵_____.
Becoming detached from spacecraft	Astronauts are taught to use a small ⁶_____ to steer back to spacecraft.

Understanding Vocabulary: Phrasal Verbs

Phrasal verbs are two-word (sometimes three-word) verbs. They consist of a verb + preposition or adverb, and have a different meaning from the original verb. With many phrasal verbs, such as *turn around*, you can easily figure out the meaning from the words. The meanings of other phrasal verbs are not so clear because they are idiomatic. For example, it's not obvious that *give up* means "stop trying." Some phrasal verbs can have different literal and idiomatic meanings. Look carefully at the parts of the phrasal verb and its context to see if you can guess its meaning before you check a dictionary.

DEFINITIONS   **A.** Look back at the reading passage. Find and write the phrasal verbs that match these definitions.

1. removed (paragraph B) _____

2. discovered (paragraph C) _____

3. performed (paragraph D) _____

4. handle; manage (paragraph D) _____

5. review (paragraph D) _____

6. faint (paragraph E) _____

7. became an adult (paragraph F) _____

COMPLETION   **B.** Circle the correct word to complete each phrasal verb.

Sunita Williams is not only a spacewalker, she is also a space runner. While on the ISS in 2007, Williams [1] **took part** *at / in / with* the Boston Marathon. Unlike runners on Earth, who had to [2] **deal** *of / with / forward* strong winds and rain during the 42-kilometer race, Williams stayed dry. She started running on a treadmill as the race [3] **kicked** *off / to / on* in Boston and the ISS circled Earth at about 28,000 kilometers an hour. Her fellow astronauts [4] **cheered** her *with / on / over*. She [5] **ended** *off / down / up* with a race time of 4 hours, 23 minutes, and 10 seconds. "I think the idea [6] **came** *out / up / away* because I'm a big proponent[1] of physical fitness," Williams told reporters during an interview.

1 If you are a **proponent** of something, you argue in favor of it.

CRITICAL THINKING Evaluating Challenges   Which aspect of space travel would be the most difficult for you to deal with? Consider the following, or add your own idea, and discuss with a partner.

living in an enclosed space   coping with weightlessness   risk of technical problems

distance from Earth   communication challenges   other: _____

VOCABULARY PRACTICE

COMPLETION   **A.** Complete the information below with words from the box. One word is extra.

accumulated   demanding   familiarize   impressive   internal   venture

Before they can ¹_____ into space, astronauts on the ISS have to undergo a very ²_____ training process. First, they have to pass a one-year course of basic training in which they learn about space technology, medical procedures, and the ³_____ workings of the ISS. They also ⁴_____ themselves with scuba diving to get used to the feeling of floating in space. After they have ⁵_____ the required number of training hours, they can be assigned to a mission.

DEFINITIONS   **B.** Use the correct form of words in the box to complete the definitions. One word is extra.

consciousness	concern	detach
impressive	pioneer	venture

1. You admire or respect something that is _____.
2. A(n) _____ is the first person to do something.
3. If something becomes _____ from something else, it separates from it.
4. If something _____ you, you feel anxious about it.
5. _____ is the normal state of being awake and aware.

> Astronauts train in a jet plane to get used to the feeling of weightlessness.

WORD PARTS   **C.** The word **familiarize** is formed using the suffix **-ize**. The suffix, meaning "cause" or "become," can be added to other words. Complete the sentences with the correct form of the words in the box.

hospital	modern	popular	social

1. Astronauts have few people to _____ with in space.
2. Returning astronauts are _____ for a short time: Being on the ISS can be physically and mentally exhausting.
3. There is a constant need to improve and _____ the ISS.
4. Astronomer Carl Sagan helped _____ astronomy with his 1980 TV show *Cosmos*.

QUIZ **A.** Match each space exploration event with a year. Then check your answers on pages 196–197.

1. _____ China launches its first manned flight in space. a. 1961
2. _____ The U.S. launches the first space shuttle, Columbia. b. 1981
3. _____ The International Space Station is established. c. 1998
4. _____ The first space tourist visits the ISS. d. 2001
5. _____ Soviet astronaut Yuri Gagarin is the first human in space. e. 2003

PREDICT **B.** What will be some important events in space travel and exploration in the future? Check your ideas as you read the passage.

THE ULTIMATE TRIP

A Although we have sent unmanned spacecraft to Mars and other parts of our solar system for **decades**, humans haven't ventured more than 650 kilometers from Earth since 1973. However, there is increasing interest in sending new missions— both robotic and manned—into space. Unlike in the past, this renewed interest is not primarily being driven by government agencies. Instead, private companies are leading today's new age of space exploration.

B Astronauts and supplies from the United States used to be transported to the ISS by NASA's space shuttles. But the space shuttle program ended in 2011. In early 2012, SpaceX, a private company based near Los Angeles, sent an unmanned rocket to the ISS. SpaceX and other private companies are now competing to **replace** the shuttle to become the ISS's main supply ship.

C Another company called Planetary Resources—which received **backing** from Google executives—has developed plans to use robotic spacecraft to mine[1] asteroids[2] for **precious** metals. One that the company hopes to find is platinum,

In this artist's impression, an unmanned probe explores a new solar system.

a metal so rare on Earth that an ounce costs $1,600. Robots will have to travel millions of kilometers to locate and mine asteroids, and this requires technology that doesn't exist yet. However, this isn't stopping companies like Planetary Resources and others from trying. They are investing millions into research, hoping to create tools that will make space mining possible. "This is the beginning of the new space age," says Dr. Mason Peck, NASA's Chief Technologist. "The energy we see now—the economic motivation to go into space—we haven't seen that before."

D For centuries, economics has driven exploration. A thousand years ago, merchants risked the dangers of the Silk Road to reach the markets of China. In the 15th century, European ships traveled to new worlds, searching less for knowledge than for gold and spices. "Historically, the driver has always been the search for **resources**," explains investor Peter Diamandis. If you want people to explore space, he says, create an economic incentive.

E Entrepreneur Elon Musk, the **founder** of SpaceX, is spending a large part of his **fortune** on his own space program. SpaceX has developed a rocket that transports cargo[3] to the ISS relatively cheaply. Musk reduced costs by creating reusable rockets—in the same way that we reuse a plane after a flight. People first thought that creating reusable rockets would be **extremely** difficult, or even impossible, but Musk knew there was no other way to keep costs down. "If we threw away airplanes after every flight," he says, "no one would fly."

F For Musk, creating reusable rockets has been part of a much bigger plan: He wants to establish a human colony on Mars. NASA has had enormous success on Mars with unmanned spacecraft, but it has yet to **launch** a manned mission. Musk says SpaceX could put astronauts on Mars within 10 years, and keep sending them for decades after that. "We can't send one little group to Mars," he says. "We have to take millions of people and lots of equipment to Mars to make it a self-**sustaining** civilization." It will be the hardest thing that humanity has ever done, but Musk thinks his company can do it and he's eager to see it happen. "It's about making life multiplanetary," he says. "It's about getting out there and exploring the stars."

1 When people **mine** for metals, they dig deep holes in the ground to extract them.

2 An **asteroid** is a rock that orbits the sun, typically found in a zone between Mars and Jupiter.

3 **Cargo** refers to the supplies a ship or plane carries.

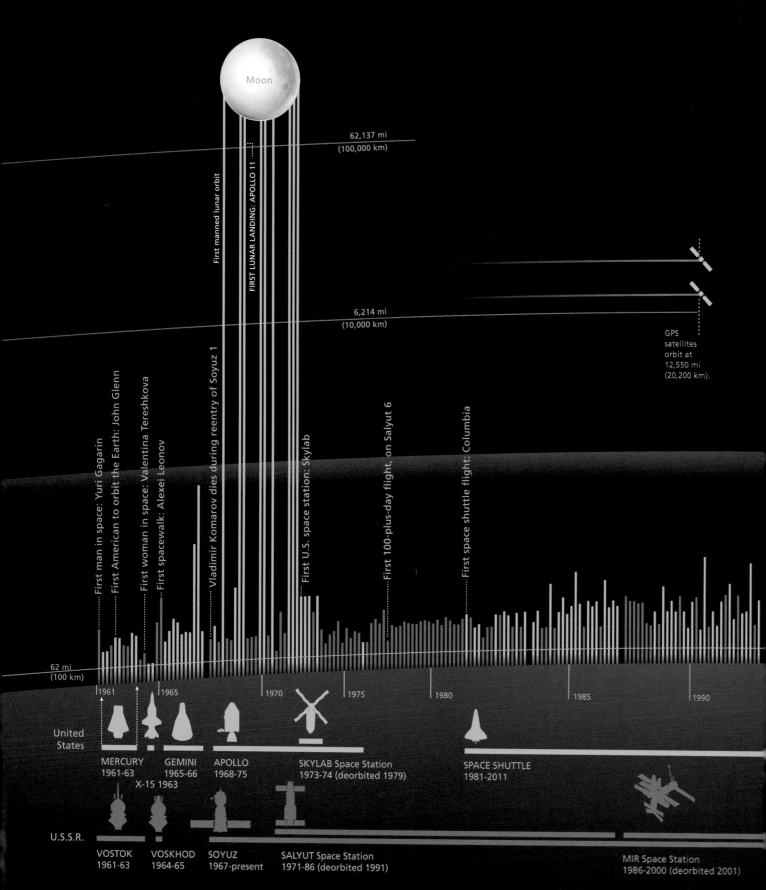

621,371 mi
(1,000,000 km)

Moon

62,137 mi
(100,000 km)

6,214 mi
(10,000 km)

GPS
satellites
orbit at
12,550 mi
(20,200 km).

First manned lunar orbit

FIRST LUNAR LANDING: APOLLO 11

First man in space: Yuri Gagarin

First American to orbit the Earth: John Glenn

First woman in space: Valentina Tereshkova

First spacewalk: Alexei Leonov

Vladimir Komarov dies during reentry of Soyuz 1

First U.S. space station: Skylab

First 100-plus-day flight, on Salyut 6

First space shuttle flight: Columbia

62 mi
(100 km)

1961   1965   1970   1975   1980   1985   1990

United
States

MERCURY
1961-63

GEMINI
1965-66
X-15 1963

APOLLO
1968-75

SKYLAB Space Station
1973-74 (deorbited 1979)

SPACE SHUTTLE
1981-2011

U.S.S.R.

VOSTOK
1961-63

VOSKHOD
1964-65

SOYUZ
1967-present

SALYUT Space Station
1971-86 (deorbited 1991)

MIR Space Station
1986-2000 (deorbited 2001)

CHARTING
THE MISSIONS

In the first 50 years of manned spaceflight, 500 men and women from some 40 countries made 276 space missions.

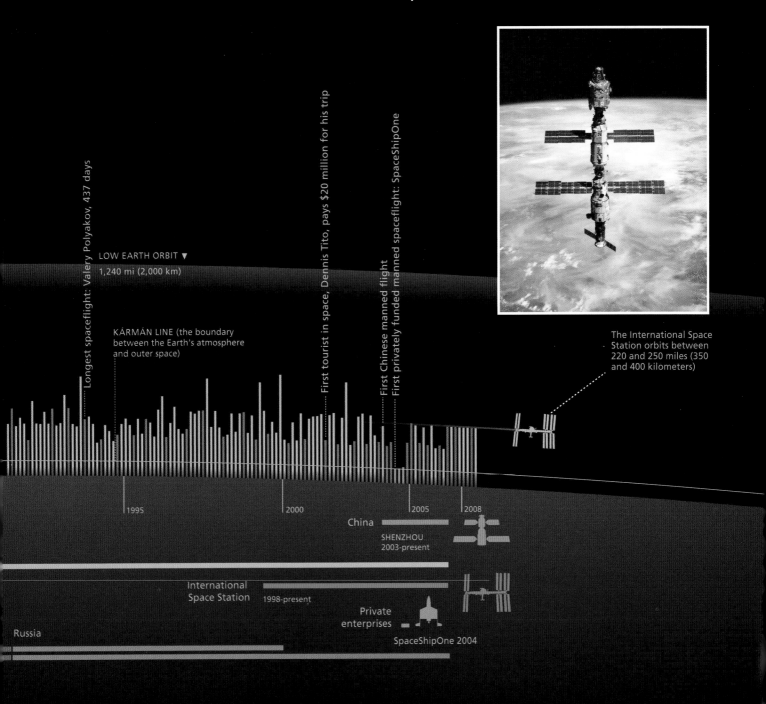

Longest spaceflight: Valery Polyakov, 437 days

LOW EARTH ORBIT ▼
1,240 mi (2,000 km)

KÁRMÁN LINE (the boundary between the Earth's atmosphere and outer space)

First tourist in space, Dennis Tito, pays $20 million for his trip

First Chinese manned flight

First privately funded manned spaceflight: SpaceShipOne

The International Space Station orbits between 220 and 250 miles (350 and 400 kilometers)

1995   2000   2005   2008

China
SHENZHOU
2003-present

International
Space Station   1998-present

Private
enterprises

SpaceShipOne 2004

Russia

READING COMPREHENSION

A. Choose the best answer for each question.

DETAIL

1. Which statement about space exploration is NOT true?

a. In 2012, a private company sent an unmanned rocket to the ISS.

b. Humans have recently traveled more than 650 kilometers from Earth.

c. There is newfound interest in manned and unmanned missions to space.

d. More and more private companies are beginning to explore space.

REFERENCE

2. What does *One* refer to in the second sentence of paragraph C?

a. one asteroid

b. one spacecraft

c. one metal

d. one reason

VOCABULARY

3. What could the word *energy* be replaced with in the last sentence of paragraph C?

a. fuel

b. enthusiasm

c. technology

d. capacity

MAIN IDEA

4. What is the main idea of paragraph D?

a. Making money has always encouraged exploration, and space exploration is no different.

b. It will take many more resources to convince people to travel to space.

c. The development of space travel has been slow due to economic reasons.

d. The search for knowledge, rather than economics, is what should drive space exploration.

DETAIL

5. What does SpaceX want to do?

a. build a space station that can replace the ISS

b. get the government's approval to transport astronauts to the ISS

c. partner with Planetary Resources to mine asteroids for platinum

d. send a manned spacecraft to Mars in order to colonize it

INTERPRETING INFOGRAPHICS

B. Are the following statements true or false according to the "Charting the Missions" infographic, or is the information not given? Circle T (true), F (false), or NG (not given).

1. There have been no manned missions to the Moon since the 1960s.   **T F NG**

2. The United States first landed on the moon during the Mercury program.   **T F NG**

3. The Soyuz program was the most expensive space program.   **T F NG**

4. Most manned missions have not gone beyond the low Earth orbit level.   **T F NG**

5. The U.S.S.R. performed the first space flight of more than 100 days.   **T F NG**

6. The United States made the most space flights between 1995 and 2005.   **T F NG**

Understanding Appositives

Appositives are nouns or noun phrases that rename or identify another noun beside them by providing additional information. They can appear at the beginning, in the middle, or at the end of a sentence, and are usually set off by commas. For example:

A former Navy pilot, Sunita Williams has performed seven spacewalks.

Sunita Williams, a former Navy pilot, is now retired as an astronaut.

However, there are some structures that appear to be appositives, but are not. An adverbial phrase at the start of a sentence, for example, gives extra information about the action of a sentence, such as its time or place.

A thousand years ago, merchants risked the dangers of the Silk Road.

ANALYZING **A.** Check (✓) the sentences that contain appositives.

☐ **1.** Neil Armstrong, the first man to walk on the moon, died in 2012.

☐ **2.** A 722-kilogram space probe, Voyager 1 was launched in 1977 to study the solar system.

☐ **3.** Several companies, hoping to take tourists into space, are taking reservations now.

☐ **4.** In 2018, China became the first country to land on the dark side of the moon.

APPLYING **B.** Label each sentence (1–3) with the correct appositive (a–c) from the box. Then check your answers in the reading passage.

> a. NASA's Chief Technologist
> b. the founder of SpaceX
> c. a private company based near Los Angeles

1. In early 2012, SpaceX, ____, sent an unmanned rocket to the ISS. (paragraph B)

2. "This is the beginning of the new space age," says Dr. Mason Peck, ____. (paragraph C)

3. Entrepreneur Elon Musk, ____, is spending a large part of his fortune on his own space program. (paragraph E)

CRITICAL THINKING Speculating

▶ Discuss with a partner. How likely do you think building a Mars space colony is?

▶ Would you be interested in going there? Why or why not?

COMPLETION   **A.**   Complete the information using words in the box. Two words are extra.

backing	decades	extremely	fortune
precious	replace	resources	sustain

Encouraged by new technologies and the potential to generate riches, many companies, such as Deep Space Industries (DSI), have created plans to mine asteroids in the coming ¹_____. There are thousands of near-Earth asteroids that contain ²_____ metals like gold and platinum. But other more basic elements such as water, nickel, and iron are also required to ³_____ a space colony and other ventures in space.

DSI's Founding CEO, David Gump, says that obtaining ⁴_____ from beyond Earth is essential for future space travel. This is because pushing through the Earth's atmosphere is ⁵_____ expensive. Some 90 percent of the weight lifted by a rocket sending a capsule to Mars is fuel. Space exploration would be much cheaper if some of the fuel could be picked up on the way. In 2015, DSI received financial ⁶_____ to start building a spacecraft that may help make its dream a reality.

△ **Japan's probe *Hayabusa* nears an asteroid.**

DEFINITIONS   **B.**   Complete the sentences. Choose the correct words.

1. When you **launch** a rocket, you _____.
   a. land it on the ground   b. build it   c. send it into the air

2. A **fortune** is a _____ money.
   a. little   b. moderate amount of   c. lot of

3. The **founder** of a business is _____.
   a. its first product   b. the person who created it   c. its original location

4. You are likely to **replace** a product if it's _____.
   a. in a store   b. very new   c. broken

COLLOCATIONS   **C.**   The words in the box are frequently used with the adjective **precious**. Complete the sentences with the correct words. One word is extra.

baby	metal	moment	stones

1. Diamonds, rubies, and emeralds are examples of precious _____.
2. While silver is considered a precious _____, gold is much more valuable.
3. For many astronauts, seeing the Earth for the first time from space is a precious _____.

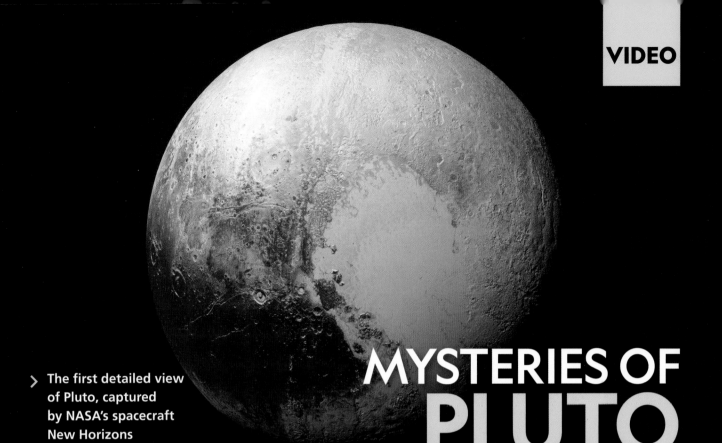

> The first detailed view of Pluto, captured by NASA's spacecraft New Horizons

MYSTERIES OF PLUTO

BEFORE YOU WATCH

DEFINITIONS **A.** Read the information. The words and phrases in **bold** appear in the video. Match the words to their definitions.

Pluto is one of thousands of objects in the Kuiper belt—a vast area of rocky **debris** that **orbits** our sun at the edge of the solar system. Home to icy worlds and frozen comets, the Kuiper belt is far too **frigid** for life to exist. But images from NASA's New Horizons probe reveal that Pluto could be geologically alive. The heat in Pluto's **core** is helping to create new ice on the surface. New Horizons is continuing to learn more about Pluto and the strange objects in the Kuiper belt.

1. **debris** •   • to travel completely around something in space

2. **orbit** •   • the center of something

3. **frigid** •   • pieces of useless or leftover material

4. **core** •   • extremely cold

PREDICT **B.** What do you know about Pluto? Circle the answers and compare your ideas with a partner.

Pluto . . .

- is classified as a *dwarf planet / moon*
- is about *two-thirds / twice* the size of Earth's moon
- takes *24.8 / 248* Earth years to orbit the sun

- has a high temperature of around *–26°C / –226°C*
- has mountains of *ice / rock* with rivers of frozen *nitrogen / water*

WHILE YOU WATCH

VIEWING   **A.** Watch the video. Check your predictions in Before You Watch B.

DETAIL   **B.** Watch the video again. Choose the best answer for each question or statement.

1. According to the video, it is so cold on Pluto because _____.

   a. the surface is covered in gases

   b. it is so far away from the sun

2. Pluto was named after the Roman god of _____.

   a. the sea   b. the underworld

3. How was Pluto classified when it was first discovered?

   a. as the ninth planet in the solar system

   b. as a moon orbiting Neptune

4. Pluto was reclassified as a dwarf planet because _____.

   a. it is too small, and is actually another planet's moon

   b. it is not able to clear debris out of its path of orbit

---

CRITICAL THINKING Synthesizing   Discuss these questions with a partner.

▶ Do you think humans will ever send manned missions to Pluto? Why or why not?

▶ Compared to going to the moon or Mars, what additional challenges might humans face going to Pluto?

VOCABULARY REVIEW

Do you remember the meanings of these words? Check (✓) the ones you know. Look back at the unit and review any words you're not sure of.

Reading A

☐ accumulate*   ☐ concern   ☐ consciousness   ☐ demanding   ☐ detached

☐ familiarize   ☐ impressive   ☐ internal*   ☐ pioneer   ☐ venture

Reading B

☐ backing   ☐ decade*   ☐ extremely   ☐ fortune   ☐ founder*

☐ launch   ☐ precious   ☐ replace   ☐ resource*   ☐ sustain*

* Academic Word List

Photo and Illustration Credits

Cover Lars Van de Goor, **3** Lars Van de Goor, **4–5** Igor Prahin/Moment/Getty Images, **7** Mark Thiessen/NGIC, **8–9** VW Pics/Universal Images Group/Getty Images, **10** Skip Brown/NGIC, **11** Riley Champine/NGIC, **12** brunosphoto/Alamy Stock Photo, **14** Aurelien Meunier/Getty Images News/Getty Images, **15** Clive Brunskill/Getty Images Sport/Getty Images, **16–17** Mark Thiessen/NGIC, **18** Jack Sullivan/Alamy Stock Photo, **21** Aurora Photos/Alamy Stock Photo, **23** Michele and Tom Grimm/Alamy Stock Photo, **24** Annie Griffiths/NGIC, **25** Annie Griffiths, **26–27** Gordon Gahan/NGIC, **28** Yoshikazu Tsuno/AFP/Getty Images, **30** David Levenson/Hulton Archive/Getty Images, **31** Mint Images – Frans Lanting/Mint Images/Getty Images, **32–33** Jodi Cobb/NGIC, **34** Thomas J. Abercrombie/NGIC, **36** Martin Puddy/Asia Images/Getty Images, **37** Brigitte Blättler/Moment Open/Getty Images, **39** Joel Sartore/NGIC, **40–41** Joel Sartore/NGIC, **42** NGM Maps/NGIC, **43** Joel Sartore/NGIC, **44** Joel Sartore/NGIC, **46** Holger Ehlers/Alamy Stock Photo, **47** Steve Winter/NGIC, **48–49** Steve Winter/NGIC, **50–51** Arco Images GmbH/Alamy Stock Photo, **53** Joel Sartore/NGIC, **54** Joel Sartore/NGIC, **55** Ami Vitale/NGIC, **57** Ezra Acayan/NurPhoto/Getty Images, **58–59** Robert Harding Picture Library/NGIC, **60** AFP/Stringer/Getty Images, **61** Digital Vision/Getty Images, **62** Salvatore Allegra Photography/Moment/Getty Images, **63** SPL/Science Source, **64** National Geographic Maps/NGIC, **66–67** Eric Hanson/NGIC, **68** James Balog/The Image Bank/Getty Images, **70** Bachkova Natalia/Shutterstock.com, **71** Hindustan Times/Getty Images, **73** Juampiter/Moment Open/Getty Images, **74–75** Sisse Brimberg/NGIC, **76** David Noton/Nature Picture Library, **78** NGIC, **80–81** Igor Prahin/Moment/Getty Images, **82–83** Alex Saberi/NGIC, **84** NGIC, **87** Rosanna U/Image Source/Getty Images, **89** Jessica Kirsh/Alamy Stock Photo, **90** (1) Shebeko/Shutterstock.com, **90** (2) OlgaKot17/Shutterstock.com, **90** (3) Katharina Osterholt/EyeEm/Getty Images, **90** (4) magnetcreative/E+/Getty Images, **90–91** (5) Fotofermer/Shutterstock.com, **90** (6) focal point/Shutterstock.com, **90–91** (7) procurator/DigitalVision Vectors/Getty Images, **90–91** (8) Smneedham/Photolibrary/Getty Images, **90** (chart) NGIC, **91** evrimertik/iStock/Getty Images Plus, **92** Mongkol Chuewong/Moment/Getty Images, **93** NinaM/Shutterstock.com, **96–97** Ariel Skelley/DigitalVision/Getty Images, **98–99** Marie-Laure Cuschi/NGIC, **102** Canovas Alvaro/Paris Match Archive/Getty Images, **103** Darren McCollester/Getty Images News/Getty Images, **105** Jim Richardson Photography/NGIC, **106** James L. Stanfield/NGIC, **108** Marion Owen/Design Pics/NGIC, **110** Panoramic Stock Images/NGIC, **111** fiftymm99/Moment Open/Getty Images, **112–113** Luca Locatelli, Institute for National Geographic/NGIC, **114** Luca Locatelli, Institute for National Geographic/NGIC, **115** Alvaro Valino/NGIC, **117** George Frey/Getty Images News/Getty Images, **119** Nick Kaloterakis, Sean McNaughton, NGM Staff; David W. Wooddell/NGIC, **121** Robert Harding Picture Library/NGIC, **122–123** James L. Stanfield/NGIC, **124** XPACIFICA/NGIC, **125** NGIC, **127** aphotostory/Shutterstock.com, **128** Gonzalo Azumendi/The Image Bank/Getty Images, **129** Mariana Bazo/Reuters, **130–131** Dominic Cram/Flickr/Getty Images, **131** NGIC, **134** Leonid Andronov/Alamy Stock Photo, **135** Emmanuel Rondeau/Alamy Stock Photo, **137** Coneyl Jay/Stone/Getty Images, **138–139** Boris Horvat/Getty Images, **140** David McNew/AFP/Getty Images, **141** Baptiste Fernandez/Icon Sport/Getty Images, **142** baranozdemir/iStock/Getty Images, **144** Carlos Osorio/Toronto Star/Getty Images, **145** Whale Research Solutions/NGIC, **146** AFP Contributor/AFP/Getty Images, **148** Stephen Barnes/Emergency Services/Alamy Stock Photo, **150** dpa picture alliance archive/Alamy Stock Photo, **151** CliqueImages/Photodisc/Getty Images, **153** Brian J. Skerry/NGIC, **154–155** Paolo Woods/NGIC, **156** Shotshop GmbH/Alamy Stock Photo, **157** Dr. Arthur W. Toga, Laboratory of Neuro Imaging at UCLA, **160–161** Andrew Suryono, **162** Frans Lanting/NGIC, **163** Kurz/laif/Redux, **166** Juergen & Christine Sohns/Minden Pictures, **167** Daniel Hertzberg/NGIC, **168** Alfred Pasieka/Science Photo Library/Getty Images, **169** Alex Segre/Alamy Stock Photo, **170–171** Jasper Juinen/Getty Images News/Getty Images, **172–173** The Starry Night, June 1889 (oil on canvas) (detail of 216295), Gogh, Vincent van (1853–90)/Museum of Modern Art, New York, USA/Bridgeman Images, **173** National Geographic Maps/NGIC, **174** Doug Pearson/AWL Images/Getty Images, **176** "Sudden Shower at Ohashi Bridge at Ataka" ("Ohashi, atake no yudachi") from the series "100 Views of Edo," 1857, pub. 1859, (aiban size, color woodblock print) (see also 167548), Hiroshige, Ando or Utagawa (1797–1858)/Fitzwilliam Museum, University of Cambridge, UK/The Bridgeman Art Library, **177** Timothy A. Clary/AFP/Getty Images, **178** Album/Alamy Stock Photo, **179** Album/Alamy Stock Photo, **180** Hayk Shalunts/Alamy Stock Photo, **181** South China Morning Post/Getty Images, **182** Lenscap/Alamy Stock Photo, **184** Paul Marotta/Getty Images Entertainment/Getty Images, **185** Pacific Press/Alamy Stock Photo, **187** NASA, **188–189** STS-116 Shuttle Crew, NASA, **190** (top) Marco Grob/NGIC, **190** NASA Photo/Alamy Stock Photo, **191** QAI Publishing/Universal Images Group/Getty Images, **193** AFP/Getty Images, **194–195** Stephan Martiniere/NGIC, **196–197** National Geographic Maps/NGIC, **197** NASA/Getty Images, **200** Akihiro Ikeshita/AFP/Getty Images, **201** NASA

NGIC = National Geographic Image Collection

Text Credits

9 Adapted from "Joy is Round," by Jeremy Berlin: NGM, February 2013, and "See Which World Cup Teams Have the Most Foreign-Born Players," by Riley D. Champine: NGM, July 2018, **16** Adapted from "Pushing the Limit," by Rick Gore: NGM, September 2000, **25** Adapted from "The Enigma of Beauty," by Cathy Newman: NGM, January 2000, **32** Adapted from "Unmasking Skin," by Joel L. Swerdlow: NGM, November 2002, **41** Adapted from "Racing to Rescue Koalas," by Mark Jenkins: NGM, May 2012, **48** Adapted from "Out of the Shadows," by Douglas H. Chadwick: NGM, June 2008, **59** Adapted from "Fuji: Japan's Sacred Summit," by Tracy Dahlby: NGM, August 2002, and "Popocatépetl: Mexico's Smoking Mountain," by A. R. Williams: NGM, January 1999, **65** Adapted from "The Next Big One," by Joel Achenbach: NGM, April 2006, **75** Adapted from "Iceland: Europe's Land of Fire, Ice, and Tourists," by Stefan Lovgren: National Geographic News, **81** Adapted from "The Five Thousand Mile Beach," by Stanley Stewart: National Geographic Traveler, March 2008, **91** Adapted from "Caffeine," by T. R. Reid: NGM, January 2005, **97** Adapted from "How Science Is Unlocking the Secrets of Addiction," by Fran Smith: NGM, September 2017, and "This is Your Brain on Nature," by Florence Williams: NGM, January 2016, **107** Adapted from "Tapped Out," by Paul Roberts: NGM, June 2008, and "Future Power: Where Will the World Get Its Next Energy Fix?," by Michael Parfit: NGM, August 2005, **113** Adapted from "The World's Most Improbable Green City," by Robert Kunzig: NGM, October 2017, **123** Adapted from "China's Ancient Lifeline," by Ian Johnson: NGM, May 2013, **130** Adapted from "Peru's Highway of Dreams," by Ted Conova: NGM, June 2003, and "Bugs Help Measure Impact of New Transoceanic Highway on Amazon," by Ker Than: National Geographic News, May 2012, **139** Adapted from "How Virtual Reality Affects Actual Reality," by Simon Worrall: National Geographic News, February 11, 2018, **146** Adapted from "The Surprising Ways Drones Are Saving Lives," by Nina Strochlic: NGM, June 2017, and "How Tiny Planes Could Revolutionize Health Care," by Christina Nunez: National Geographic News, July 7, 2017, **155** Adapted from "Beyond the Brain," by James Shreeve: NGM, March 2005, and "Remember This," by Joshua Foer: NGM, November 2007, **161** Adapted from "Minds of Their Own," by Virginia Morell: NGM, March 2008, and "Almost Human," by Mary Roach: NGM, April 2008, **171** Adapted from "Vincent Van Gogh: Lullaby in Color," by Joel L. Swerdlow: NGM, October 1997, **178** Adapted from "6 Female Artists Who Turned Modern Art On Its Head," by Elaina Zachos: NGM, April 2018, **189** Adapted from "Spacewalker," by Pat Walters: NGM, October 2013, **194** Adapted from "Crazy Far," by Tim Folger: NGM, January 2013

NGM = National Geographic Magazine

Acknowledgments

The Authors and Publisher would like to thank the following teaching professionals for their valuable feedback during the development of the series.

Akiko Hagiwara, Tokyo University of Pharmacy and Life Sciences; **Albert Lehner**, University of Fukui; **Alexander Cameron**, Kyushu Sangyo University; **Amira Traish**, University of Sharjah; **Andrés López**, Colégio José Max León; **Andrew Gallacher**, Kyushu Sangyo University; **Angelica Hernandez**, Liceo San Agustin; **Angus Painter**, Fukuoka University; **Anouchka Rachelson**, Miami Dade College; **Ari Hayakawa**, Aoyama Gakuin University; **Atsuko Otsuki**, Senshu University; **Ayako Hisatsune**, Kanazawa Institute of Technology; **Bogdan Pavliy**, Toyama University of International Studies; **Braden Chase**, The Braden Chase Company; **Brian J. Damm**, Kanda Institute of Foreign Languages; **Carol Friend**, Mercer County Community College; **Catherine Yu**, CNC Language School; **Chad Godfrey**, Saitama Medical University; **Cheng-hao Weng**, SMIC Private School; **Chisako Nakamura**, Ryukoku University; **Chiyo Myojin**, Kochi University of Technology; **Chris Valvona**, Okinawa Christian College; **Claire DeFord**, Olympic College; **Davi Sukses**, Sutomo 1; **David Farnell**, Fukuoka University; **David Johnson**, Kyushu Sangyo University; **Debbie Sou**, Kwong Tai Middle School; **Devin Ferreira**, University of Central Florida; **Eden Kaiser**, Framingham State University; **Ellie Park**, CNC Language School; **Elvis Bartra García**, Corporación Educativa Continental; **Emiko Yamada**, Westgate Corporation; **Eri Tamura**, Ishikawa Prefectural University; **Fadwa Sleiman**, University of Sharjah; **Frank Gutsche**, Tohoku University; **Frank Lin**, Guangzhou Tufu Culture; **Gavin Young**, Iwate University; **Gerry Landers**, GA Tech Language Institute; **Ghada Ahmed**, University of Bahrain; **Grace Choi**, Grace English School; **Greg Bevan**, Fukuoka University; **Gregg McNabb**, Shizuoka Institute of Science and Technology; **Helen Roland**, Miami Dade College; **Hiroshi Ohashi**, Kyushu University; **Hiroyo Yoshida**, Toyo University; **Hojin Song**, GloLink Education; **Jackie Bae**, Plato Language School; **Jade Wong**, Belilios Public School; **James McCarron**, Chiba University; **Jane Kirsch**, INTO George Mason University; **Jenay Seymore**, Hong Ik University; **John Appleby**, Kanda Institute of Foreign Languages; **John Nevara**, Kagoshima University; **Jonathan Bronson**, Approach International Student Center; **Joseph Zhou**, UUabc; **Junjun Zhou**, Menaul School; **Kaori Yamamoto**; **Katarina Zorkic**, Rosemead College; **Keiko Miyagawa**, Meiji University; **Kevin Tang**, Ritsumeikan Asia Pacific University; **Kieran Julian**, Kanda Institute of Foreign Languages; **Kim Kawashima**, Olympic College; **Kyle Kumataka**, Ritsumeikan Asia Pacific University; **Kyosuke Shimamura**, Kurume University; **Lance Stilp**, Ritsumeikan Asia Pacific University; **Li Zhaoli**, Weifang No.7 Middle School; **Liza Armstrong**, University of Missouri; **Lucas Pignolet**, Ritsumeikan Asia Pacific University; **Luke Harrington**, Chiba University; **M. Lee**, KCC; **Maiko Berger**, Ritsumeikan Asia Pacific University; **Mandy Kan**, CNEC Christian College; **Mari Nakamura**, English Square; **Masako Kikukawa**, Doshisha University; **Matthew Fraser**, Westgate Corporation; **Mayuko Matsunuma**, Seijo University; **Michiko Imai**, Aichi University; **Mei-ho Chiu**, Soochow University; **Melissa Potts**, ELS Berkeley; **Monica Espinoza**, Torrance Adult School; **Ms. Manassara Riensumettharadol**, Kasetsart University; **My Uyen Tran**, Ho Chi Minh City University of Foreign Languages and Information Technology; **Narahiko Inoue**, Kyushu University; **Neil Witkin**, Kyushu Sangyo University; **Olesya Shatunova**, Kanagawa University; **Patricia Fiene**, Midwestern Career College; **Patricia Nation**, Miami Dade College; **Patrick John Johnston**, Ritsumeikan Asia Pacific University; **Paul Hansen**, Hokkaido University; **Paula Snyder**, University of Missouri-Columbia; **Reiko Kachi**, Aichi University / Chukyo University; **Robert Dykes**, Jin-ai University; **Rosanna Bird**, Approach International Student Center; **Ryo Takahira**, Kurume Fusetsu High School; **Samuel Taylor**, Kyushu Sangyo University; **Sandra Stein**, American University of Kuwait; **Sara Sulko**, University of Missouri; **Serena Lo**, Wong Shiu Chi Secondary School; **Shin Okada**, Osaka University; **Silvana Carlini**, Colégio Agostiniano Mendel; **Silvia Yafai**, ADVETI: Applied Tech High School; **Stella Millikan**, Fukuoka Women's University; **Summer Webb**, University of Colorado Boulder; **Susumu Hiramatsu**, Okayama University; **Suzanne Littlewood**, Zayed University; **Takako Kuwayama**, Kansai University; **Takashi Urabe**, Aoyama-Gakuin University; **Teo Kim**, OROMedu; **Tim Chambers**; **Toshiya Tanaka**, Kyushu University; **Trevor Holster**, Fukuoka University; **Wakako Takinami**, Tottori University; **Wayne Malcolm**, Fukui University of Technology; **Wendy Wish**, Valencia College; **Xingwu Chen**, Xueersi-TAL; **Yin Wang**, TAL Education Group; **Yohei Murayama**, Kagoshima University; **Yoko Sakurai**, Aichi University; **Yoko Sato**, Tokyo University of Agriculture and Technology; **Yoon-Ji Ahn**, Daks Education; **Yu-Lim Im**, Daks Education; **Yuriko Ueda**, Ryukoku University; **Yvonne Hodnett**, Australian College of Kuwait; **Yvonne Johnson**, UWCSEA Dover

These words are used in *Reading Explorer* to describe various reading and critical thinking skills.

Analyze   to study a text in detail, e.g., to identify key points, similarities, and differences

Apply   to think about how an idea might be useful in other ways, e.g., solutions to a problem

Classify   to arrange things in groups or categories, based on their characteristics

Evaluate   to examine different sides of an issue, e.g., reasons for and against something

Infer   to "read between the lines"—information the writer expresses indirectly

Interpret   to think about what a writer means by a certain phrase or expression

Justify   to give reasons for a personal opinion, belief, or decision

Rank   to put things in order based on criteria, e.g., size or importance

Reflect   to think deeply about what a writer is saying and how it compares with your own views

Relate   to consider how ideas in a text connect with your own personal experience

Scan   to look through a text to find particular words or information

Skim   to look at a text quickly to get an overall understanding of its main idea

Summarize to give a brief statement of the main points of a text

Synthesize to use information from more than one source to make a judgment or comparison

INDEX OF EXAM QUESTION TYPES

The activities in *Reading Explorer, Third Edition* provide comprehensive practice of several question types that feature in standardized tests such as TOEFL® and IELTS.

Common Question Types	IELTS	TOEFL®	Page(s)
Multiple choice (main idea, detail, reference, inference, vocabulary, paraphrasing)	✓	✓	12, 18, 28, 34, 44, 52, 61, 68, 77, 84, 93, 100, 109, 116, 126, 132, 142, 148, 157, 164, 174, 182, 191, 198
Completion (notes, diagram, chart)	✓		18, 78, 94, 100, 126, 132, 157, 158, 191
Completion (summary)	✓	✓	14, 20, 36, 46, 63, 68, 86, 102, 111, 118, 127, 128, 134, 144, 150, 159, 166, 176, 184, 193, 200
Short answer	✓		34, 142, 148
Matching headings / information to paragraphs	✓		28, 44, 61, 116, 182
Categorizing (matching features)	✓	✓	12, 18, 85, 93, 109
True / False / Not Given	✓		77, 88, 152, 198

The following tips will help you become a more successful reader.

1 Preview the text

Before you start reading a text, it's important to have some idea of the overall topic. Look at the title, photos, captions, and any maps or infographics. Skim the text quickly, and scan for any key words before reading in detail (see pages 58 and 64).

2 Use vocabulary strategies

Here are some strategies to use if you find a word or phrase you're not sure of (see page 45):

- **Use context** to guess the meaning of new words.
- **Look at word parts** (e.g., prefixes and suffixes) to work out what a word means.
- **Look for definitions** of new words within the reading passage itself.
- **Use a dictionary** if you need, but be careful to identify the correct definition.

3 Take notes

Note-taking helps you identify the main ideas and details within a text. It also helps you stay focused while reading. Try different ways of organizing your notes, and decide on a method that best suits you (see pages 35, 53, 62).

4 Infer information

Not everything is stated directly within a text. Use your own knowledge, and clues in the text, to make your own inferences and "read between the lines" (see pages 133 and 175).

5 Make connections

As you read, look for words that help you understand how different ideas connect. For example:

- **synonyms** that show connections between sentences and paragraphs (see pages 149, 165, 183)
- transition words that describe **contrasting ideas** (see page 101)

6 Read critically

Ask yourself questions as you read a text. For example, if the author presents a point of view, is enough supporting evidence provided? Is the evidence reliable? Does the author give a balanced argument? (see pages 29, 94, 110)

7 Create a summary

Creating a summary is a great way to check your understanding of a text. It also makes it easier to remember the main points. You can summarize in different ways based on the type of text. For example:

- **timelines** (see page 126)
- **T-charts** (see page 94, 132)
- **Venn diagrams** (see page 18)
- **concept maps** (see page 158)
- **research summaries** (see page 100)
- **visual summaries** (see page 78)